Pugs

DIANNE BOURGEOIS

Pugs

Project Team
Editor: Heather Russell-Revesz
Copy Editor: Ann Fusz
Interior Design: Leah Lococo Ltd. and Stephanie Krautheim
Design Layout: Angela Stanford

First published in the United Kingdom in 2009 by

Interpet Publishing
Vincent Lane
Dorking
Surrey
RH4 3YX

United Kingdom Editorial Team
Claire Cullinan
Nicola Parker
Hannah Turner

ISBN 9781 84286 211 7

Printed and bound in China.

This book has been published with the intent to provide accurate and authoritative information in regard to the subject matter within. While every reasonable precaution has been taken in preparation of this book, the author and publisher expressly disclaim responsibility for any errors, omissions, or adverse effects arising from the use or application of the information contained herein. The techniques and suggestions are used at the reader's discretion and are not to be considered a substitute for veterinary care. If you suspect a medical problem consult your veterinarian

Promoting responsible pet ownership

INTERPET
PUBLISHING

www.interpet.co.uk

Table of **Contents**

Chapter 1

Why I Adore
MY Pug

Once you let a Pug into your life it will never be the same. This charming and comical breed is unlike many typical dogs because he was bred for one sole purpose—as a companion for humans. Be forewarned, the Pug takes his duty to provide companionship very seriously. In fact, many Pug owners refer to their little darlings as "Velcro dogs."s

Queen Mary II popularised the Pug in England.

If companionship is what you are seeking, then the Pug fits the bill. However, the Pug's definition of companionship is to spend every waking and sleeping moment with his owner. The Pug does best in a home where a family member is available most of the day. Although this little dog enjoys the company of other Pugs and pets, his main focus is always on the human members of his family. In return for your devotion to this furry family member, the Pug will shower you with kisses, keep your lap warm, entertain you with his comedic skills, and let you know that you are the most important person on the planet.

History of the Pug

The Pug breed originated in China. It was one of the small breeds, along with the Pekingese, who were treasured and pampered by Chinese royalty. Pugs were also favoured as pets by Buddhists monks in Tibetan monasteries. It is not known exactly how old the breed is, but there are references to short-nosed, pug-like dogs that date back to 400 B.C.E. These ancestors would be somewhat different in appearance from the modern day Pug, due to various breeding programmes through the millennia.

Coming West

Theories abound as to how the Pug made its way from the East to the West. The most likely scenario is that the little dogs were brought to Holland by Dutch or Portuguese merchants who traded in China. William, Prince of Orange is credited with bringing the Pug from Holland to England when he arrived in 1688. The following year, he and his wife ascended to the throne of England as joint sovereigns, becoming William III and Mary II. The new queen was also devoted to the breed, which popularised the Pug in England.

It is not surprising that William III would have Pugs. His great grandfather, William the Silent, King of Holland, had declared the Pug the official dog of the House of Orange in the 16th century after his life was saved by his faithful Pug, Pompey. At that time, Holland was at war with Spain. While William slept, Spanish soldiers silently crept into his camp with the intention of assassinating him. Though they avoided detection by the guards, Pompey the Pug alerted his master to the danger by barking, waking William and allowing him to escape.

Fortune's Secret

The Pug's popularity spread to other European countries during the 18th century. The most famous Pug from that time is Fortune, the beloved pet of Josephine, the future wife of Napoleon Bonaparte, emperor of France. Legend has it that Fortune, who was accustomed to sleeping in his mistress' bed, tried to "protect" Josephine on her wedding night and bit Napoleon on the leg. Another story has Napoleon sending love notes to Josephine while she was in prison by hiding them in Fortune's dog collar. This tale, though romantic, overlooks historical accounts that suggest that she did not meet Napoleon until after her internment in Carmes, and it may have been Josephine's children who sent the secret messages in Fortune's collar. While we may never know which

The Expert Knows

The Dreaded Shed

Pugs are notorious for shedding. Owners have been known to match their colour choice of clothing and furniture to the colour of their fawn or black Pug. Double-coats shed more than single-coats; double-coats are found more often in the fawn Pug. Lint rollers and vaccum cleaners become a part of every Pug owner's life—but the benefits are worth it!

version is true, this fact remains clear—Fortune the Pug lives on in Pug history.

The Pug's head is large with deep wrinkles and a black mask.

In Great Britain

The first organised dog show in Great Britain was held in 1859, but only Pointers and Setters were entered. By 1870, participants in showing felt that a controlling body was necessary to set basic rules regarding dog shows. In April of 1873 the Kennel Club was founded. The Club's objective is to promote the general improvement of dogs and to protect and promote the dog's varied roles in society. Although the Kennel Club marks its beginning as 1873, registration records only go back as far as 1908, at which time hundreds of Pugs were already registered; so, there is no way to know the name of the first registered Pug.

Physical Characteristics of the Pug

Throughout the world, national kennel clubs set standards for each breed of dog called the "breed standard." The Pug standard describes the ideal Pug's physical build, gait, and temperament. This standard provides a guide for breeders who are dedicated to improving their breed with each generation. Reputable breeders will strive to match the Pug standard as closely as possible. Pugs who win championships in the show ring are the dogs who have come closest to the Pug standard.

Size

The Pug is the largest breed in the Toy Group. According to the breed standard, his weight should be from 14 to 18 pounds (6.3 to 8.1 kg). He is a solid dog, and the Latin phrase *multum in parvo* is often used to describe the Pug. This phrase, which translates as "a lot in a little," is perfect for the Pug, since he is a lot of dog in a compact package (or more popularly, "a lot of dog in a little space").

Head

The most prominent feature of the Pug is the head, which is large with deep wrinkles and a black mask. Large prominent dark brown eyes are in contrast to the short muzzle. A dog with a short muzzle or flat face is called a brachycephalic breed.

The ears are black and as soft as velvet. Either the button or rose shaped

8

Pugs

ear is allowed for show dogs. Button ears fold forward and lie against the skull. The rose variety folds further back and may reveal the ear opening.

Did you know that the Pug has a beauty mark? The Pug sports a black mole on each cheek. And that interesting design on his forehead is called a thumb mark or diamond. It is made by vertical wrinkles, and may be enhanced by black hair in the fawn variety. This mark is also called the "prince mark" as it resembles the Chinese character for prince.

Body

The physical build of the Pug is described as "cobby." Viewed from the side, the Pug should have a square shape rather than rectangular. Remember, this little dog should be compact. The tail sits high on the Pug's rump and is distinguished by the curl. A double curl is considered very desirable for showing. The black line down his back is called the "trace."

Colour

The Pug is either fawn-coloured with a black mask and black ears, or he is solid black. The fawn coat is usually golden or cream-coloured. If the coat is more orange in tone, it is called "apricot". The rare "silver" is a very light, clear coat.

Coat

Some Pugs are double-coated, an attribute more common in fawns than blacks. Double-coats shed more than single-coats, but the reality is that all Pugs shed. The shedding factor can be a serious issue for people with allergies or who prefer their homes spotlessly clean. This should be considered carefully before acquiring a Pug.

My own Pug is a double-coated fawn, and her coat is luxuriously soft. The down side is that she is a super-shedder. I've referred to her as the destroyer of vacuum cleaners due to the sheer number that have burnt out over the

Pugs come in black and fawn colours.

The Pug has beauty and brains.

Pugs

years in a futile attempt to rid my home of Pug hair. Personally, I have to admit that the joy she brings me far outweighs the nuisance of shedding.

SENIOR DOG TIP

When Is My Pug Considered a Senior?

Small dogs have a longer life span and enter their senior years at a later age than larger breeds. The Pug can live between 12 to 15 years and enters his senior years around eight years of age. Although he won't have the energy of a young pup, the older Pug is often quite active and still retains the loving personality and funny antics common to the breed.

Pug Personality

The Pug has one of the most delightful temperaments in the dog world. Though his face may appear to express constant concern, this is a happy breed. The Pug revels in being the centre of attention and will do almost anything to get it—often of a comical nature.

The Pug requires a lot of attention from his human. Whether you have one Pug or a house full of Pugs, this breed will need—and demand—your attention. If you prefer a dog who will be content to amuse himself or lie

A Pug Named Hamlet?

The distinguished actor Paul Winfield, who appeared in many movies and TV shows, including "Touched by an Angel" and "LA Law," was a Pug-o-phile. He bred and showed black Pugs for many decades. Mr. Winfield had seven Pugs at the time of his death; each one named after a Shakespearian character.

Some other famous people who have owned Pugs include: Ted Danson, Jenna Elfman, Christine Elise, Lena Horne, Billy Joel, Carol Kane, Jacqueline Kennedy, Chris Kirkpatrick of 'Nsync, Jason Priestly, Mickey Rourke, Silvia Sidney, Tori Spelling, Maura Tierney, Valentino, Goran Visnijc, Andy Warhol, and Tom Welling.

Royalty who have owned Pugs include: Josephine Bonaparte (the wife of Napoleon), Marie Antoinette, William III and Mary II, Queen Victoria, Queen Charlotte (the wife of George III), the Duke and Duchess of Windsor, Prince Rainier and Princess Grace of Monaco, and the Dowager Empress Cixi (T'zu Hsi) of China.

quietly in a corner of the room, the Pug is not for you. This dog is an interactive housemate.

Intelligence

The Pug has beauty and brains. One of the best descriptions of the Pug is from The Kennel Club in Britain. Their Pug standard lists the characteristics of the Pug as having "Great charm, dignity and intelligence." Talk to your Pug—you'll notice his ears moving up and down as if trying to catch the words he knows. He'll cock his head if you use an unfamiliar word. Through patience, repetition, and understanding each other's body language, you should have very little trouble communicating. Of course, that doesn't mean he'll always listen—the Pug can be quite stubborn.

My Pug has learned to understand many English words, phrases, and sentences over the years. As a result, my family members began spelling words out if we didn't want her to know what we were talking about— but my Pug has now figured out many of the words we commonly spell out! Interact with your Pug, and give him as much one-on-one attention as you can—you'll soon find out just how smart he really is.

Because this breed is intelligent, calm and patient training with a firm voice is the most effective method. Positive reinforcement with food treats works especially well, as the Pug is very food driven. The Pug also enjoys attention, and he will aim to please if the training is fun for both him and his owner. The Pug can display a stubborn streak, but he can learn new behaviours if his owner maintains consistency and a patient demeanour.

The friendly nature of the Pug makes him a good companion for a child.

The Pug can give an Academy Award-worthy performance of a starving dog and make his care-giver feel like a villain out of a Charles Dickens' novel. I speak from experience. I made the error of giving in and ended up with a happy but overweight Pug. I have since learned my lesson. My girl is now trim though she still shoots me "the look" that begs, "Mommy, I am starving. That meal I had five minutes ago wasn't enough." Is it hard to ignore her? You bet. But the upside is that she will be healthier and live longer—the best gift of all.

The Price of Fame

It is fun to watch Pugs in movies such as *Milo and Otis* and the *Men in Black*, but there is also a serious drawback when a dog breed appears in the media—the popularity of the breed soars. Many people will buy a popular dog breed without considering if it is a good match for the family. Unfortunately, many of the dogs bought during the height of popularity will eventually be surrendered to an animal shelter or to a breed rescue group. That is why it's so important to do your research before deciding on what breed is right for you.

He Lives to Eat!

For the Pug, life is a banquet, and this includes not only his daily adventures but his appetite for food. It is the rare Pug who will turn up his nose at a morsel of food (or a plateful for that matter). As a result, the Pug is prone to obesity, which can lead to serious health problems and shorten his life span. Therefore, it is very important for his family to monitor his food intake including both meals and snacks. A healthy diet and exercise will maintain your Pug's general health.

The friendly nature of the Pug makes him a good companion for a child. Keep in mind that although the Pug is a sturdy dog, he is not built for rough-housing or playing outside all day. He will, however, be a devoted and loving best friend. With very young or immature children, the Pug is at risk for injury (especially eye injuries). For the safety of both child and Pug, young children should never be left unattended with a pet. Even the most docile Pug may feel the need to defend himself against the poking and prodding of a curious or mischievous youngster.

Prior to acquiring a Pug or any other dog breed, parents should consider their child's interests and activity level. Choosing a breed because it starred in a popular movie or because the neighbour has one can lead to unrealistic expectations resulting in disappointment. An athletic child may be better off with a larger, more active dog. It is important to match the breed of dog with both the family's and the child's lifestyle. The pros and cons of owning a dog should be discussed with the child. Remember, at the other end of doggie devotion is the need for a pooper-scooper.

Children of all ages need to be taught appropriate behaviour and respect for their pets. Pugs and other animals are not disposable toys that can be cast aside when interest in them wanes. Acquiring a Pug can be a 12 to 15 year commitment that requires daily care, including feeding, walks, and potty breaks.

With the best intentions, children often promise to care for a pet but don't follow through. As an adult, the ultimate responsibility for your pet lies with you. Pugs and children naturally gravitate toward each other. In exchange for taking on the duties associated with pet care, a deep and priceless bond can form between the child and Pug.

Chapter 2

The Stuff of
Everyday Life

Before you bring your new Pug home, you should
have all the supplies you need to make the
transition to his new life easier for the both of
you. Remember, your home is a whole new world
to your Pug, and he has to learn which areas
and items are for him. By preparing ahead, you
can avoid the stress and frenzy of last minute
shopping for necessary dog products. After all, you
will want to spend those precious first hours and
days welcoming your new furry friend into your
home and heart.

Bed

Dog beds can be a simple round or rectangular style or take the shape of a nest, chair, sofa, or "people bed." If you want to indulge your dog, four-poster or elegant canopied beds are available. As for size, your Pug should be able to stretch out comfortably on his bed. For cleanliness, many pet beds have zippered covers which can be removed and washed.

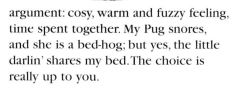

A dog bed can provide a nice comfy place for your Pug.

The crate can also serve as a sleeping area. Of course, the Pug usually has his own preference where to sleep—your bed. There are arguments both for and against letting your dog sleep with you in your bed. Intellectually I agree with the *against* argument: health, cleanliness, drawing the line between your space and his space. Emotionally I agree with the *for* argument: cosy, warm and fuzzy feeling, time spent together. My Pug snores, and she is a bed-hog; but yes, the little darlin' shares my bed. The choice is really up to you.

Cleaning Equipment

You'll need to keep lint/hair removal sheets on hand. These sheets are sticky on one side and come in squares

A harness instead of a collar may be right for your Pug.

or wrapped on a roller. Use the lint sheets to remove the Pug hair from your clothing and furniture. I often wipe down guests with one before they leave my house.

A vacuum cleaner isn't usually listed as a necessary dog supply, but if you plan to get a Pug it would behoove you to get a decent vacuum cleaner. There's no getting around it—Pugs shed.

Collar and Harness

A dog collar is an essential item for your dog. However, many dog owners don't realise that there is an alternative to the classic collar—it's called a harness, and it can be a lifesaver for many Pug owners. Some Pugs have breathing difficulties that can be aggravated by a collar, so the harness, which falls around the dog's body and not the neck, can be a better choice.

There is debate among Pug owners about whether it is best to use a collar or a harness, since it is easier to train a dog with a collar and lead; but for health reasons the harness may work best for your Pug. My own Pug did fine with a collar when she was a puppy, but I eventually had to go with the harness. As she grew into an adult, her shoulders filled out but her head remained fairly small, and she was able to work her head out of the collar.

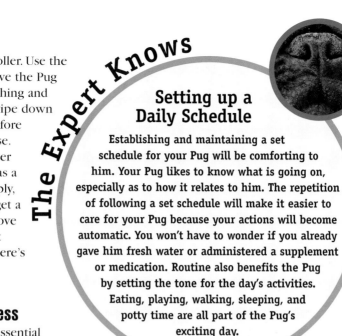

The Expert Knows

Setting up a Daily Schedule

Establishing and maintaining a set schedule for your Pug will be comforting to him. Your Pug likes to know what is going on, especially as to how it relates to him. The repetition of following a set schedule will make it easier to care for your Pug because your actions will become automatic. You won't have to wonder if you already gave him fresh water or administered a supplement or medication. Routine also benefits the Pug by setting the tone for the day's activities. Eating, playing, walking, sleeping, and potty time are all part of the Pug's exciting day.

If you decide to go with a collar, you'll find a large assortment of styles in nylon and leather. Avoid the metal collars, often referred to as choke chains, as they are inappropriate for the Pug and could do damage to his sensitive throat area.

Harnesses are made of nylon or leather. Some nylon harnesses have colour-coordinating leashes and collars available. The ID tags can be attached to the harness if your Pug doesn't wear a collar—simply put the tags on the same loop where you attach the lead.

Remove the collar or harness when your Pug is inside, especially if he will be unattended. Collars can be especially dangerous if caught on dog pens or furniture.

SENIOR DOG TIP

Keep a Routine

When an older Pug is available for adoption, chances are that he spent many years in his previous home. Pugs prefer routine so it can be quite unsettling for an older Pug to be placed in a new environment. In the beginning, follow his previous schedule (if it is known). If he arrives with his own belongings (e.g., toys, blanket, bed) the familiar smell will be comforting to him. Supervising him as he navigates your home can double as a bonding experience. An older Pug should adapt fairly quickly to his new family if he feels safe and loved.

Pugs

Whether you choose a collar or a harness, make sure to get the right size for your Pug's build. The collar or harness should not be too loose or too tight. Make sure you can fit two fingers in between the device and your Pug.

Crate

A crate has many useful functions for your dog. Although it is cage-like in appearance, the crate provides your Pug with a comfy room of his own—it's the modern version of a wolf den. The crate provides a safe place to contain your Pug when necessary and is also a useful tool in housetraining and behaviour modification. What it is *not*, however, is a prison. It is not meant to be used all day or as a punishment for problem behaviours. (See Chapter 6 for more information.)

Crates come in various sizes, shapes, colours, and styles. Wire crates are the most common type used in the home. There are also travel crates for the car and crates that comply with airline specifications. As for choosing a size, your Pug should be able to stand up and turn around as well as lie down comfortably in the crate. However, you don't want a crate that is too large as it could sabotage housetraining. Crate mats are available to make the crate floor more comfortable, and many crates come with a water bowl attachment.

Doggy Door

A doggy door allows a housetrained dog to go outside to toilet in the garden and then return inside, all by himself. These special doors are installed in the door or wall of the house and usually have an insert or lock for times you want to keep your dog inside or prevent other animals from entering.

Food and Water Bowls

There are a several types of food and water bowls available for your Pug. Though most bowls are sold individually, there are fancy food and water bowl sets available, and some even come in an elevated stand. The bowls are commonly made of stainless steel, ceramic, or plastic and come in various sizes. The 32 ounce bowl is fine for the average Pug, but smaller Pugs or puppies may do better with a smaller-sized bowl. Personally, I prefer stainless steel bowls as they are easier to sterilise. (Plastic bowls have a tendency to harbour bacteria.) My Pug has an easier time eating out bowls that are "V" shaped inside (slanted toward the middle), but other Pug owners I know say their Pugs do well with bowls that are "U" shaped (straight sides). If you find your Pug struggling to eat out of his bowl, search for a different size or shape until you find the one that's most comfortable for him. Some Pugs, including my own, must have their food dishes elevated to assist in properly digesting their food.

Gate

Dog gates are just like baby gates and are used for the same purpose—to restrict access to certain rooms or areas. A gate can provide a safety barrier to a set of stairs or a room that's not puppy-proofed. One nice feature about the gate is that even if your Pug can't be in the same room, at least he can see you and you can communicate with him.

Grooming Equipment

Even though he is small and short-haired, the Pug is not low maintenance when it comes to grooming. His coat sheds. His nose roll, wrinkles, ears, and teeth need to be cleaned. His eyes require attention too. And those nails seem to sprout overnight even after a recent clipping. For bathing and grooming your Pug, you will need to have the right equipment and products. See

A doggy door can be useful for a housetrained Pug.

Exercise!

The Pug is prone to becoming overweight, and exercise is as important as a balanced diet. Exercise, such as a daily walk, does as much for your Pug's mental health as physical health because the sights and sounds provide mental stimulation. It relieves boredom which is one of the major causes of canine misbehaviour or depression. Besides keeping him fit, the Pug will enjoy playing with you or checking out the neighbourhood when taking a walk. So grab that lead and start walking—exercise time may very well be a highlight in your Pug's day.

Chapter 4 for a list of basic grooming supplies and how to use them on your Pug.

Housetraining Equipment

Even if your new Pug is already housetrained, be prepared for accidents. Whether the Pug is a puppy, an adult, or a senior, finding himself in a totally new environment with strangers can be confusing and stressful. He will need to learn where he is expected to go potty. No matter how well-trained your dog is or how long he has lived with you, he can have an accident when he is not feeling well or confined inside for too long a time without a potty break.

- **Cleaning products**. Always keep a cleaning product on hand that will rid your flooring or furniture of doggy messes, stains, and odour. Pet supply companies make cleaning products specifically for cleaning up after pets. Regular cleaners don't always remove the smell, and if the odour is not eliminated, it becomes the pet version of a lavatory sign.

- **Pooper scooper**. A pooper scooper is anything that can pick up a mess—it can be a plastic scoop you purchase from the pet shop or even a plastic baggy. The plastic baggy is a convenient way to clean up after your Pug in public places. You can buy doggy baggies from pet supply companies or use sandwich bags. With your hand protected inside the bag, pick up the mess and then turn the bag inside out and dispose of it in a proper receptacle. Remember to be a good neighbour, and always pick up after your Pug.

- **Indoor housetraining items**. If you plan on training your Pug to go potty indoors, decide whether you will use puppy pads (tray optional but I recommend it), a doggy litter box, or the old standby, newspaper. Whichever method you use, have plenty of it on hand.

- **Belly band**. If you have a male Pug who marks indoors or is incontinent, you can wrap a belly band around him. A belly band, also called a male wrap, is the male dog version of a diaper. It looks rather like a cummerbund around his back end. Replaceable pads fit inside the wrap.

- **Piddle pants**. For the female Pug in season or who is incontinent, there is a diaper garment also known as piddle pants. This too has replaceable pads that fit inside.

A gate, food bowls, and toys are just a few of the supplies your Pug will need.

Identification

Dogs love to explore and run free, and the Pug is no exception. Be aware that the Pug is a breed that is inconsistent with the "Come" command when he is outside, as he tends to get distracted by all the sights, sounds, and smells. It is for that reason the Pug should always be on lead or in a safe fenced-in area when outside. But if he does get loose and wanders off or runs away, how will you get him back?

ID Tags

The identification tag is the primary way a stranger can identify your dog and return him to you. Anytime you are outside or travelling with your Pug, he should have identification on his collar or harness in case he wanders off. At the very least, the tag should display his name and your phone number. Some tags allow space for your address or other pertinent information.

Tattoo and Microchip

There may be times you remove your Pug's collar in the house, and he accidentally sneaks out; or there's a chance the person who finds him might remove his collar and tags. What can you do then? Many dog owners turn to tattooing or microchipping as a permanent way to identify their dogs.

Tattoos have been used in

shoulder area beneath the dog's neck. Each microchip has a unique number, which when scanned provides identifying information on the dog, such as the owner's contact information and the dog's veterinarian. Most animal control officers, shelters, and veterinarians have the equipment to scan a lost dog's microchip.

If your Pug escapes without his ID tags or if a dog thief removes the tags, the importance of the microchip comes into play. If your Pug is found, the microchip will identify you as the true owner and provide contact information so that the dog can be returned.

Your veterinarian can microchip your Pug. Microchipping is sometimes offered at a pet or dog function at a reduced price, but make sure the person performing the microchipping is a qualified veterinarian, veterinarian technician, or animal control officer.

Even though I live in a rural area, I was pleased to learn

the world of dog shows for many years. An identifying number, such as your phone number, can be tattooed onto your Pug's belly or inside of the thigh on a back leg.

Microchips have become quite popular in the past few years. A microchip about the size of a grain of rice is injected into the top of the

Identifying Your Pug

The Control of Dogs Order 1992 stipulates that any dog in a public place must wear a collar with the name and address (including postcode) of the owner engraved or written on it. Your telephone number is optional, but advisable. You can incur a large fine if you dog does not wear identification. ID tags are available from most hardware shops or through your veterinarian's surgery.

lead in the ring, which does not require a collar—it is one piece with a loop on the end which slips over the dog's head.

The standard nylon or leather lead is a good choice for walking the Pug. The nylon lead can usually be colour-coordinated with the collar or harness for the fashionable Pug. There is also a retractable lead available (similar in concept to a retractable tape measure) which allows a longer length of lead for the dog—but it may provide more length than a Pug needs. Be aware that there have been reports of injuries sustained by pet owners using the retractable lead when the lead snapped back. As with any product, read the safety precautions and follow the directions for proper use if you choose a retractable lead.

from my local animal control officer that microchip scanners are available in many small rural towns as well as large urban cities. Now that my little descendant of the ancient Chinese Pug carries 21st century technology inside her, I like to call her "RoboPug."

Lead

The lead is available in an array of colours and styles in nylon or leather. The most common lengths are four and six feet (1.2 and 1.8 m). The size and style you choose will depend on the purpose of the lead; will it be used for walks, obedience training, or for the show ring? Professional dog trainers have varying opinions on what type of lead and collar they prefer during training. Show dog handlers use a show

Toys

There are so many dog toys available, it boggles the mind. Your first consideration is getting a toy that is safe for your Pug. Choose one that is size appropriate. Inspect it for safety.

Pugs

FAMILY-FRIENDLY TIP

Children and Responsibility

A Pug is a living being and to place him in the sole care of child is not a good idea. You risk your pet not getting the care and attention he requires. Before acquiring a Pug, a parent should carefully consider if he or she has the time and desire to care for the Pug if the child does not follow through or loses interest in the dog after the novelty has worn off. How much responsibility a child can truly commit to is dependent on the age and maturity of that child. Children can still be involved by assisting the parent or a mature older child in the Pug's care.

Pug has a preference for a certain type of plush material, and no matter what the toy represents—bear, duck, monkey—it must have extensions—arms, legs, ears—to suck on or gently chew. She saves her more aggressive chewing for her nylon bone.

X-pen

"X-pen" is short for exercise pen (although it is really too small to provide much exercising.) The x-pen is used in a similar way to a child's playpen. It can be used indoors or outdoors and provides your dog a greater amount of freedom to move around than a crate. The x-pen is easy to transport and set up when you travel with your Pug.

Beware of toys that are poorly made, too flimsy, or have features that can be easily torn off. Remember, your Pug loves to eat, and if he can break off part of a toy for a snack, he will. As you get to know your Pug's chewing habits and chewing strength, you will have a better idea of what toys are best for him.

Some Pugs develop a preference for certain types of toys; others aren't so fussy. And then there are Pugs who aren't interested in toys at all. My own

There are many fun toys available for your Pug.

Ideally, from the Pug's perspective anyway, there should be someone home the majority of the day so that he can fulfil his companionship duties. Of course, this is just not possible for Pug owners who work outside the home. But there are times when it is absolutely necessary to have a person who can look in on your Pug while you are at work or gone for the day. Puppies and some senior Pugs need frequent potty breaks. Pugs on a medication schedule may need medicine administered at specific times throughout the day. If you are not able to go home on your lunch break or unable to leave work for any reason, then you need to consider other options.

Do you have a responsible relative, friend, or neighbour who is willing to care for your Pug during the day? Are you comfortable having this person attend to your Pug and would he or she be equally comfortable attending to your Pug alone? If the answer is no, consider these alternatives: a dog walker, a pet sitter, or doggy day care.

If your Pug just needs potty breaks and/or exercise, a dog walker may provide the solution. A pet sitting service provides one or more home visits during the day, which include walking the dog, as well as personalised services such as administering medication and giving your Pug the one-on-one human interaction that he craves. Doggy day care takes your Pug out of the home to a doggy-friendly facility that provides interaction and socialisation with other dogs as well as with people.

Before conferring responsibility for your Pug on an individual or organisation, it is wise to verify his or her reputation. Ask for references. Talk to dog owners, veterinarians, trainers, breeders, and pet shop personnel to find out if he or she has heard anything positive or negative about the service you are interested in using.

When interviewing a service, be clear about what you expect, but also understand what the service is willing to offer or not offer. This is a partnership to care for your beloved pet. Mutual respect and clear expectations for both parties will make it a good experience.

Chapter 3

Good Eating

Opinions vary on which diet is best for the Pug. There are several options available. You can choose to go with a commercial food, home-cooking, or a raw diet, depending on your (and your Pug's) preference. Whichever option you decide on, your Pug should have his own doggy diet—not foods created from human recipes or table scraps.

Keep it Safe

Certain foods are toxic to dogs such as chocolate, grapes, raisins, onions, macadamia nuts, and foods containing the substitute sweetener, Xylitol. Due to their size, small dogs like the Pug are more likely to experience a severe reaction if they ingest a toxic substance. However, any dog regardless of size, can have a severe and deadly reaction to toxins.

Changing Foods

If your Pug comes from a reputable source, you will most likely be advised to keep him on the same diet when you bring him home. If you decide to change your Pug's diet, whether it is a minor change (one brand of dry food to another) or a more radical change (commercial diet to a raw food diet), you should do it gradually to prevent digestive upset. As an example, let's say that you want to change the brand of dry food that you give to your Pug. For the first cycle, about three to five days, his daily meal amount should be 3/4 of the old food and 1/4 of the new food. The next cycle divide the food half and half. The third cycle is 3/4 of the new food and 1/4 of the old food. By the fourth cycle, your Pug should be adjusted to the new food.

A Balanced Diet

It is important to feed your Pug a balanced diet that meets his nutritional needs for optimum health. Probably the most important, and most overlooked, nutrient that the Pug needs is water. Water is essential to maintain proper functioning on the cellular level. Your Pug should always have fresh water available to keep him hydrated and healthy. Hot weather, exercise, and overexcitement that lead to panting will increase his need for water. While some foods do contain water, the amount will depend on the type of food and won't be enough to keep him hydrated. So keep those water bowls filled!

Here are some other nutrients essential to your Pug's health:

- **Proteins**. Proteins are molecules made up of amino acids, which are necessary for growth and maintenance on the cellular level.
- **Carbohydrates**. "Carbs" include starches and sugars along with fibre, which help the intestines.

28

FAMILY-FRIENDLY TIP

Feeding Tips

If your child is too young to feed the dog alone, have the youngster assist you with your Pug's meal preparation to the degree that he or she is capable. This will instil the sense of responsibility that comes with pet ownership. As for snacks, it will be easier for a child to feed the Pug by hand if the Pug sits calmly rather than jumps to grab the treat. Teach your child to give the "Sit" command to your Pug prior to giving the treat.

It is important to feed your Pug a balanced diet.

• **Minerals.** Minerals help keep bones and teeth healthy, maintain fluid balance, and influence metabolic functioning. Minerals include calcium, phosphorous, potassium, magnesium, sodium, zinc, copper, iron, iodine and selenium.

A balanced diet contains a combination of these various nutrients. The percentage that comprises the total daily requirement can vary depending on the dog's age, activity level, and metabolism. This is why commercial dog foods now offer different food products for the three life stages (puppy, adult, senior) and different activity levels (active or overweight). This is also why it's important to do your research if you decided to go with a home-cooked or raw diet.

• **Fats**. Fats are a concentrated form of energy and also provide stored energy.
• **Fatty acids**. Omega-6 and omega-3 fatty acids can heal inflammation in the joints, skin, kidneys, and intestines. Linoleic and arachidonic acids, which are part of the omega-6 family, are essential fatty acids that have a structural role in cell membranes.
• **Vitamins**. Vitamins maintain metabolic functioning. Fat-soluble vitamins include vitamins A, D, E, and K. Water soluble vitamins include vitamins B and C.

Commercial Foods

Commercial foods are a convenient way to feed your pet. These foods are ready-made, and figuring out the right balance of nutrients that your dog needs is already done for you. Once you determine the energy needs of your Pug, such as puppy versus adult or active versus overweight, you can purchase a food that is geared for that energy level. You may still have to adjust the recommended daily amount that appears on the products label, as it is usually too much for the Pug breed. Most breeders and veterinarians advise using a high-quality commercial food product with a good reputation

What About Supplements?

A balanced diet may preclude the need for supplements in a healthy Pug. However, there are situations in which a supplement is beneficial. There are supplements geared to preventing or alleviating various health problems, maintaining well-being, or improving a feature such as the dog's coat. Some supplements are added to the main meal while others are administered separately. Supplements in tasty tablet form can be used as one of your Pug's daily treats. Always check with your veterinarian before giving your Pug any supplements.

for providing a complete and balanced diet.

Tinned Food

Tinned dog food is approximately 75 percent moisture. The main ingredient may be meat-based or a cereal grain. The true amount of meat that the tin contains can be deciphered by how it is advertised on the label (see section on "Reading Food Labels" below).

Tinned food is easily digestible and usually quite appealing to dogs. A tinned food label that reads "complete and balanced" should provide the nutrition a dog needs.

As tinned dog food contains more water than dry or semi-moist, it is a good choice if you need to get more water into your Pug. Some people will even mix a small amount of tinned food in with kibble.

Tinned dog food is typically more expensive than other types of dog food. Be aware that tinned dog food is too soft to provide the dental benefits of crunchy dry food in maintaining healthy teeth. However, a dog with chewing problems including few or no teeth will find the tinned dog food easier to eat.

Dry Food

Dry dog food, also called kibble, may be made from cereal grains, animal and poultry meats, and various by-products. Dry foods contain about 10 percent

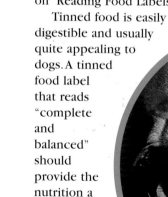

Kibble is the most popular form of dog food.

moisture.

The benefit of dry food is that it is less expensive than tinned and has a longer shelf life. Another advantage is that many of the toy breeds, including the Pug, are prone to dental problems, and the hardness of dry kibble may be better for the teeth.

Semi-moist Food

Semi-moist dog food contains 25 to 30 percent moisture and is typically more digestible than dry food. Dogs tend to prefer the taste of semi-moist food over kibble, and it is also more pleasing to the human eye as it tends to mimic the appearance of people food. (However, I've never met a Pug who cared about what his food looked like!) Your Pug is more interested in quantity than quality, whether it is in appearance or nutritional value.

Semi-moist food is more expensive than dry food and contains ingredients to prevent spoilage. These ingredients often include high levels of sugar, which can contribute to dental problems in dogs.

Reading Food Labels

Food labels must contain certain information to enable the consumer to know what he or she is buying. The label must include the product name and the manufacturer. It also must state its nutritional purpose and adequacy which is reflected in statements such as "a complete and balanced puppy food" or "complete and balanced adult dog food". The label also must provide the weight,

list of ingredients, and a guaranteed analysis. That said, interpreting the label can be difficult if you don't know the code and sometimes even if you do. Personally, I prefer a good mystery novel.

If you feed your dog only one type of food such as dry or tinned, choose products that are labelled as *complete and balanced.* If the label does not contain that magic phrase, your Pug may need supplements to meet his nutritional needs.

Phrasing is everything in interpreting dog food labels. Don't assume that a product contains a large percentage of an ingredient such a beef just because the word *beef* is

FAMILY-FRIENDLY TIP

Senior Nutritional Needs

Older dogs are prone to weight gain when their activity and exercise levels decrease. The nutritional needs of a senior may change, and the daily amount that he is fed may need to be adjusted based on his overall health. The condition of the teeth and the ability to chew must also be taken into consideration as to what type of food is easiest to eat.

required percentage of that ingredient drops to 25 percent. A label that reads "dog formula with beef," with the operative word being *formula*, lowers the minimum percentage to 3 percent. Add the word *flavour* after the ingredient and it can be less than 3 percent. Therefore, a label that reads "chicken flavoured dog food" may actually contain less than 3 percent chicken.

The ingredient list on the label is in a specific order based on the weight of each ingredient in descending order. The first few will give you a good idea of the basic make up of the recipe. If your Pug has allergies to certain foods then reading the food label is mandatory. Read the entire list of ingredients to ensure that none of the offending foods are part of the recipe.

The guaranteed analysis provides the minimum crude protein, minimum crude fat, maximum crude fibre, and maximum moisture that the food contains.

mentioned on the label. The phrasing on the label dictates the minimum percentage required of the advertised ingredient. Strap on your seatbelt; we are going for a wild ride into the realm of food labels.

A label that uses a stand alone word such as beef, chicken or fish, which may read as "beef dog food" or "chicken for dogs" indicates that the product contain at least 70 percent of that ingredient. Add the word *dinner* or *platter* such as "beef dinner" or "chicken platter" and the minimum

Food labels usually have a weight chart to determine the daily amount to feed a pet. If you use the amount recommended for your Pug's weight, you may actually over-feed him which can lead to obesity.

Noncommercial Foods

As an alternative to commercial foods, you can prepare your Pug's meals yourself with fresh ingredients. Some dog owners cook their pet's food, and others are proponents of a raw diet.

Home-cooked Diet

A benefit of the home-cooked diet is that your Pug is getting fresh foods. Also, this type of diet can be tailor-made for the Pug with allergies or other ailments that call for the addition of or avoidance of certain foods.

A home-cooked diet for a dog does *not* mean sharing the family meal with him—he has his own nutritional needs. Care must be taken to choose ingredients that will offer your Pug a balanced diet. You will need to investigate your Pug's specific nutritional needs and learn which foods will provide that balance. Your veterinarian or someone who specialises in animal nutrition can guide you in this process. You will also need to be aware of what foods are toxic to dogs.

Of course, the home-cooked diet is more time consuming than opening up a tin of dog food or measuring out kibble. It is also more expensive. Some pet owners supplement a commercial food diet with home-cooked foods while others only provide home-cooked meals. For those who enjoy cooking, they can add that special ingredient to their Pug's bowl—love.

A note about serving home-cooked food to your Pug: *never give a cooked bone to your dog—it could splinter and harm him when swallowed.*

Raw Diet

The most popular raw diet is the "BARF diet," which stands for Biologically Appropriate Raw Foods or Bones and Raw Food diet. The theory is to recreate or mimic the diet of dogs in the wild. Your dog's early ancestors were not the pampered pooches

Puppies need to be fed more frequently than adults.

Feeding Chart

The following chart is a general example of the Pug's feeding schedule. The daily total amount is divided evenly among the feeding times. For example: If your Pug requires one cup a day and you feed him twice a day, each meal will consist of 1/2 cup.

Be aware that individual Pugs may have different nutritional needs than what is posted in a general chart. The labels on commercial dog food recommend meal amounts based on a dog's weight, but the listed amount is usually far too much to feed a Pug.

To determine how much to feed an individual Pug, factors such as age, size, activity level, metabolism, and health need to be considered. Ask your Pug's breeder or veterinarian to help you ascertain the amount and type of food that is best for your Pug. You still may have to fine-tune your Pug's diet so that he does not become overweight or underweight, but getting advice from a professional who knows your Pug is a good place to start.

Sample Feeding Schedule for Each Phase of Your Pug's Life

Age	Times per Day	Amount	Best Food
Puppies (3 to 6 months)	3-4	3/4 to 1 cup	puppy diet
Adolescents (6 months to 1 year)	2	1 to 1 1/2 cups	adult diet
Active Adult (1 to 8 years)	2	1 cup	adult diet
Sedenary Adults (1 to 8 years)	2	2/3 cup	light/low fat diet
Seniors (8 years and up)	2	2/3 cup	senior or light diet

we know today. Their food supply depended on what they could hunt and what plant life was edible. Even today, feral dogs exist that feed in the same way as their doggy ancestors.

Some people choose to home cook for their Pug.

The BARF diet consists of raw vegetables and meat (including bones). If you choose this diet, just like with home-cooking, you will need to investigate which foods provide the proper combination of nutrients for your Pug's specific needs.

The raw diet can be a controversial subject among vets, breeders, and dog people in general. Proponents of the BARF diet claim that it is the most natural way to feed your dog, and the health benefits outweigh the effort it takes to provide this diet to your furry companion. Opponents of the raw diet claim that as dogs evolved into companions, the type of food that is best for them has changed. New information on the pros and cons of the raw diet are continually being published. Look for the most current research so that you can decide for yourself if this diet is right for your Pug.

When Should I Feed My Pug?

There are two methods of when to feed your Pug—free feeding or scheduled feeding. Free feeding is the term used when the daily food amount is available for the dog to eat throughout the day at his own pace. I

would not recommend free feeding this breed, as I have never known a Pug to turn down available food. If his entire daily food allotment is put out all at once, I guarantee that it will all disappear within minutes. Scheduled feeding times are far more practical and healthier for the Pug breed.

It is common for adult Pugs to be fed their meal either once or twice a day. For owners who prefer feeding their Pugs twice a day, the recommended daily food amount is divided in half for each meal. Personally, I prefer feeding my own Pug twice a day to spread out the joy of feasting. Homes with multiple Pugs or pets may find that feeding once a day is more practical. Whichever method you decide upon, be consistent with the feeding time.

Treat Tips

Treats should be handed out judiciously for the sake of your Pug's health. Also take into consideration the type of treat given, as well as how many or how often. Is it high in calories and fat or is it a healthier alternative? Many vegetables—like carrot sticks—can be used as treats. Consider scheduling snack times over the course of the day to avoid overfeeding treats to your Pug. If your Pug is on a supplement in tablet form, use it as a treat. Most supplements are made to be appealing and tasty. If your Pug is on medication, even a pill hidden in a small piece of cheese or peanut butter should be counted as part of the daily treat allotment.

36

Obesity

Unfortunately, the Pug is a breed prone to obesity. Obesity increases the risk of your Pug developing health problems, such as hypertension, heart disease, orthopaedic problems, diabetes, cancer, neurological problems, and skin disease. Being overweight can also aggravate existing issues and increase the risk of infections. For example, a Pug with hip or knee joint problems will be far more uncomfortable or have increased pain if he is overweight.

One reason for this breed's propensity towards obesity is his food drive. Pugs love to eat, and it is hard for many owners to ignore that pleading look for just one more treat. To avoid obesity in your dog, keep him on a balanced diet, limit him to healthy snacks, and make sure he receives daily exercise. With the exception of typical "puppy energy" in his first few months of life, the Pug is fairly laid back. But just like high-energy breeds, he still needs exercise to help control his weight and promote good health. Get him moving, whether it is a walk down the street or running around in the garden. And the Pug is small enough to coax him into a running game in the house during inclement weather.

The hardest part of avoiding obesity is limiting food intake, especially snacks. Some Pugs are experts at begging or employing "the look" that many people find hard to resist. Your Pug needs to learn from the start that *you* decide feeding time, not him.

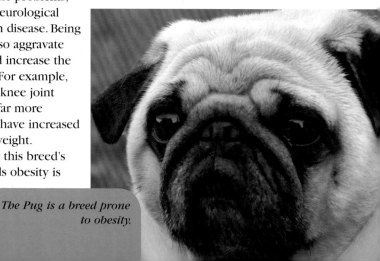

The Pug is a breed prone to obesity.

subsequent dog retains his own position. This is to discourage jealousy and a canine turf war. Of course, this may be easier said than done if you have a pack of Pugs jumping up and down at your feet. However, training and patience will make mealtime and snack time much more pleasant in the long run.

3 The Pug needs to be taught that begging is inappropriate and will not be rewarded. This has to be one of the most difficult challenges for the Pug owner. It can be hard to resist those big brown pleading eyes and the patented Pug look that screams, "I'm starving!"—even though he just had his meal five minutes ago. There are two good reasons to ignore "the look"—it teaches your Pug that begging does not work and, even more importantly, lowers the risk of having an obese and unhealthy Pug.

4 In addition to teaching your Pug not to beg for his own food, he must be taught not to beg for your food either. Nothing is more annoying than having a dog beg at the dinner table. If you hope to change this behavior, never give in and share your food with your Pug. Train him to lie down quietly, perhaps with a chew toy to keep him occupied. Put him in his crate for a time out if he is unable to calm down and behave. Remember, the crate is for training, not punishment, so calmly put him in with a chew toy and praise him when he settles down.

5 Bear in mind that even the best-trained Pug may have a relapse of table manners when the thought of food is just too enticing. Be patient and don't give in.

Table Manners

The Pug is notorious for his love of food. The sound of kibble rolling around in a measuring cup, the whirl of a tin opener, the opening of the refrigerator door, or the clink of the doggy-cookie jar lid can send the Pug into a wild frenzy of anticipation. Unless you want to be assaulted every time your Pug is given food, he must be taught the Puggie version of table manners.

1 Teach your Pug that he must sit and wait while you prepare his meal or get his treat. He still may quiver and his eyes glaze over with ecstasy, but as long he remains in the sitting position, praise him for being a good boy.

2 If you have more than one dog, they should be fed in the order that they came into your home as furry family members. The reasoning behind this is to reassure the first acquired dog that he is still in the number one position in the pack and that each

Chapter 4

Looking Good

Despite his size and short-coat the Pug is *not* low maintenance in the grooming department. This breed sheds—a lot—and if he is double-coated, he will shed even more. His nose roll and wrinkles accumulate debris that if not cleaned out can lead to infection. His ears need to be kept clean of excess wax and dirt. His eyes may require lubrication. The Pug's nails are notorious for their fast growth and being, well, hard as nails! The toy breeds are more prone to dental problems, and the Pug is no exception.

W hen I am out and about with my Pug, admiring strangers frequently comment on how easy it must be for me to keep her so clean. While I'm tempted to laugh,

Basic Grooming Supplies

The following is a list of the basic grooming tools and supplies you'll need to keep your Pug looking good:
- Wire slicker brush
- Rubber-toothed brush
- Flea comb
- Dog shampoo
- Absorbent towel
- Mineral oil
- Cotton balls
- Nail clippers and/or nail grinder
- Emery board
- Styptic powder
- Cotton swabs
- Ear cleaning pads
- Ear cleaning liquid
- Eye wash
- Pre-moistened bath wipes
- Dog toothpaste and toothbrush or oral rinse

instead I use this as an opportunity to educate them about Pug care, even if it is only to say that Pugs shed a lot and require frequent brushing. I've even heard "I don't have time for all this stuff" when I suggest wrinkle cleaning to owners of Pugs who have a smell emanating from their faces. Pug owners who've done their research and understand how much grooming time this breed needs will have a much better attitude toward grooming duties. And, a positive attitude toward grooming time can double as bonding time with your Pug.

Coat and Skin Care

The Pug standard describes the breed's coat as "Fine, smooth, soft, short and glossy, neither hard nor woolly." The Pug may have a double-coat or a single coat. A double-coated Pug will have a top coat that is firm and a soft undercoat. A single-coated Pug does not have the soft undercoat. Fawn Pugs tend to be double-coated and black Pugs usually have a single coat.

Brushing

Brushing your Pug will help keep his coat clean and healthy. Not only will brushing remove dirt and dead hair, but it distributes natural oils that keep his coat shiny. Brushing will also reduce shedding.

A wire slicker brush will remove a lot of loose hair and is the common choice for heavy duty brushing. If your Pug is double-coated, you can also use an undercoat rake to supplement regular brushing. An

undercoat rake only loosens and removes the undercoat hair, so you'll still need to use the wire slicker brush.

The grooming session will be easier if you use a grooming table or stand your Pug on a sturdy table-high surface. For the latter, place a non-slip mat on it for your Pug's safety.

Start brushing just below the back of the head and work down. Be extra gentle around the head and legs and wherever the hair is sparse such as the belly area. On the areas where the coat is thick, brushing against the hair may help loosen the dead strands, but for the most part, brush in the direction of the hair to keep your Pug's coat looking neat.

How often you brush your Pug depends on his coat, but the average is once a week. A double-coated Pug will shed more heavily and requires more frequent brushing. For in-between care, there are brushes made with rubber bristles which offer a gentler grooming than the slicker brush and give your Pug a relaxing massage while picking up stray hair. These brushes may have a strap which fits over your hand or be worn like a glove.

Lint sheets can remove dog hair from your clothing and furniture after the grooming session is finished.

Flea Comb

A flea comb is narrow and has very fine teeth that will reveal if your Pug has fleas. If the comb runs through clean, no fleas. If dark spots appear on the comb, there is a flea circus in town and your Pug is the circus tent.

42

How often you check your Pug for fleas will depend on the flea season in your area and how frequently your Pug is exposed to a potential flea problem. Some Pugs may need to be checked daily, while once a week will suffice for others. Also check your Pug for fleas if he has attended a gathering with other dogs. See Chapter 5 for information on dealing with fleas.

Bathing

Bathing your Pug will keep him both clean and comfortable. A bath will clean your Pug more thoroughly than if you just rely on brushing. Tender and hairless areas that cannot be brushed also need to be kept clean, and a bath is a good way to do this.

Individual Pugs have different bathing schedules which may be monthly or a few months apart. How frequently a Pug needs a bath will depend on his lifestyle—does he tend to remain clean, or is his favourite hobby rolling around in something disgusting? Is he a neatnik like Felix Unger or a slob like Oscar Madison? Regardless of his schedule, if he looks dirty or smells funny, it is time for a bath.

Your Pug can be bathed in the bath or in a sink that is large enough to accommodate his size. Cover the bottom of the bath or sink with a rubber mat for traction. Or, you can purchase a bath made specifically for bathing dogs.

Prior to the bath, put a drop of mineral oil into each eye. This protects them from damage that could be caused by the bath products. Also, put a cotton ball in each ear to prevent

Do I Need a Grooming Table?

A grooming table is an absolute necessity for people who are involved in the dog show world, but pet owners are less likely to own one. Pug owners may think that acquiring a grooming table is an unnecessary expense for such a small dog, but many people have found them useful. The Pug requires a frequent regimen of brushing, toenail clipping, and cleaning out all of his nooks and crannies. A grooming table will facilitate this process while also safely restraining your Pug. The grooming table also acts as a visual cue that it is grooming time. There are smaller, less-expensive grooming tables available for the pet owner who is not a professional groomer or involved in showing.

water from getting into the ear canal.

Use a gentle shampoo made for dogs. Special shampoos are available that target specific problems; for example, oatmeal shampoo is often used to relieve itching, and there are medicated shampoos to attack problems such as fleas.

Before wetting your Pug, make sure the water is at a warm and comfortable temperature, not hot or cold. Wet him thoroughly starting at the neck, moving across his back, and then work downwards. If you are using a spray attachment, do not use it on your Pug's face. Apply the shampoo according to the manufacturer's directions. Begin lathering the shampoo at the neck and work across and downward. Be careful not get water or shampoo in his eyes.

Rinse thoroughly beginning again at the neck. Continue rinsing until the water is clear of shampoo. It's important to rinse thoroughly—if shampoo residue remains, it could dull the coat or cause skin irritations.

Towel dry your Pug with an absorbent towel so that he is as dry as possible before you let him go. Then he

Looking Good

Make sure you get all the shampoo out of your Pug's coat.

can finish "air drying" either inside or, if it is a warm and sunny day, outside. Blow drying your Pug is not recommended due to his delicate eyes and sensitivity to heat. If you absolutely need to hasten the drying process with a blow dryer, keep it on the lowest setting, and don't hold the blow dryer too long in one spot or you could burn your Pug.

44

If your Pug needs just a little freshening up between bath sessions, you can clean him with a pre-moistened doggy bath wipe—the canine version of a sponge bath.

While many owners choose to bathe their Pug themselves, others choose a professional groomer. Not only will the groomer bathe your Pug, he or she will also clip his nails and trim any excess hair from between his toes or on his backside.

Nose Roll and Wrinkles

The Pug's nose roll and wrinkles must be cleaned to avoid infection. If the nose roll gives off a bad smell that does not disappear after cleaning, or if it appears red and/or swollen, see your veterinarian as the nose roll may be infected.

Some Pugs may need just an occasional cleaning while others need a daily cleaning. It depends on how

frequently and how much debris tends to collect in his nooks and crannies.

The Pug's nose roll and wrinkles can be cleansed with a damp thin soft cloth, tissue, cotton ball, cotton swab, or a pre-moistened doggy bath wipe. Dampening the cloth or tissue will enable you to remove any debris more easily. Make sure the area is dry when you are finished. If the inside of the nose roll appears irritated, you can put a little petroleum jelly in it.

My own Pug needs her nose roll checked daily, especially after a meal. I prefer the thin doggy bath wipes, which allows me to clean my Pug's nose roll more thoroughly. I cut the wipes in half because a half of a wipe is just the right size to clean all my Pug's facial nooks and crannies during her morning beauty regimen.

Ear Care

The Pug may develop an ear infection if excess wax or debris is allowed to accumulate. Some Pugs have a more frequent build up than others and may need to be checked daily or weekly. If your Pug is scratching around his ears, check them immediately for dirt, wax, or ear mites. Reddish brown or black spots may indicate ear mites which will need to be treated by your veterinarian.

The ears should be checked for debris by gently wiping the outer ear with a soft tissue, cotton ball, or an ear cleansing pad. *Do not push any material into the ear canal.* Leave in-depth inspections to your veterinarian. If there appears to be a lot of debris, discharge, or a bad smell, a trip to the veterinarian is in order.

There are various ear cleansers on the market, including small wipes or pads for the outside of the ear to a liquid form for cleaning within the ear. Liquid ear cleaners may be packaged with a bottle of a drying agent to prevent moisture from lingering in the ear. Ear drying agents can also be purchased separately. There are products for general cleaning and medicated products that target specific problems such as ear mites. Always check with your veterinarian to see if these products are appropriate for your Pug.

Eye Care

The Pug's large eyes are vulnerable to eye injury so it wise to inspect them each day. Foreign particles that settle in the eyes can cause scratches and increase the potential for permanent damage. The Pug's own hair or eyelashes can also rub against the eye. Therefore, it is important to keep the Pug's eyes clean and free from any irritants.

Depending on the Pug, he may just need a gentle wipe around the eye area if debris forms; or he may need an eye wash in the form of eye drops. If the eyes have any discharge use a soft damp tissue to gently remove it, but don't touch the eye itself.

If you suspect eye problems in your Pug, take him to the vet. Your veterinarian can determine if

The Expert Knows

Time to Bond

Grooming time should not be perceived as a chore but as an opportunity to bond with your Pug. Talk to your Pug as if the two of you are having the greatest time of your lives. Make him feel safe and loved. Never let your Pug associate grooming with fear. Use a firm voice, but do not yell and appear angry or impatient. Even if your Pug still doesn't like to be groomed, your happy voice will get his full attention and interest.

Looking Good

SENIOR DOG TIP

Grooming the Senior Pug

Care should always be taken when grooming the Pug to prevent injury or unnecessary discomfort—even more so with a senior. The Pug who has entered his senior years may have acquired some aches and pains and is now more sensitive to touch. Be extra gentle. He also may not be as limber or as steady as he used to be. If he is elevated on a table or other surface for grooming, make sure that he is safe and cannot fall off.

your Pug's eyes are healthy or if he has developed dry eye or another condition that requires eye drops, a lubricant, or other medication. You may even be referred to a veterinary ophthalmologist for further tests or treatment.

Nail Care

Nail trimming is often the most dreaded aspect of grooming, for both Pug and Pug owner alike. Even if you have a groomer or a veterinary technician cut your Pug's nails, chances are you will still have to trim them yourself in between visits.

Pug nails tend to grow very fast. If left untrimmed, the nails may grow at a downward angle below paw level making it difficult to walk. Untrimmed nails can also grow in a curled angle back into the paws. This obviously creates a very painful situation for the dog and interferes with the ability to walk.

How often a Pug's nails need to be trimmed can vary depending on individual growth rate and the surfaces the Pug walks on. Exteriors such as a concrete pavements and roads can help grind a dog's toenails down, as opposed to soft surfaces like grass.

Dog nail clippers in the shape of pliers are the most common nail care tool. If your Pug is a squirmy fellow, you may find a nail grinder easier to control than the nail clippers. An emery board can smooth out any rough edges left after the nails have been trimmed.

If you bathe your Pug yourself, trim the nails after his bath, since they will be softer and easier to trim. Many Pugs dislike having their toes touched so they may squirm, pull their paws away, or try to escape the clutches of the person holding the nail clippers or grinder. For this reason, it is preferable to place your Pug on a grooming table for nail trimming. If you don't have a grooming table, you can substitute any sturdy elevated surface such a counter top or kitchen table, but be sure to place a non-slip mat on it for your Pug's safety. Some owners are able to hold their Pugs in their laps for a trim, but this is not easy for

most owners.

When trimming your Pug's nails, it is important to just cut the tip off the nail and avoid cutting the quick. The quick is the vein that runs through the nail—it contains nerves and is painful if cut. On dogs with white nails, the quick is the pink line running through the middle of the nail. Unfortunately, most Pugs have black nails, making it difficult (if not impossible) to see the quick. Carefully cut just a little off at a time. Always keep styptic powder on hand to stop the bleeding if you should accidentally cut the quick.

Stay calm and be patient while trimming your Pug's nails. Talk to your Pug as if this is a pleasant activity. Offer a treat as a distraction or a reward.

In between trimmings, handle your Pug's paws often so that he gets used to the touch. Doing this won't guarantee that every Pug will readily accept a nail trimming, but it may lessen his anxiety.

Dental Care

When you consider that the Pug has 42 permanent teeth jam-packed into his small mouth, it should be no surprise that he is prone to dental problems. A major dental issue for the brachycephalic breeds such as the Pug is overcrowding of the teeth. When the teeth are overcrowded, it allows plaque to build up more easily. This in turn can lead to gingivitis (inflammation of the gums). If the gingivitis is left untreated and the accompanying bacteria are allowed to proliferate, it can escalate into periodontal disease and result in tooth loss.

Dental cleaning is very important because a serious dental problem can lead to more than just tooth loss or gum disease. The bacteria in the mouth can get into the bloodstream and adversely affect the heart, kidneys, and liver, and even lead to serious disease of these organs. This danger is especially acute if the dog has a pre-existing medical condition that makes certain organs more vulnerable.

Brushing your dog's teeth is the

FAMILY-FRIENDLY TIP

Kids Can Help

An older or mature child can learn to brush the Pug and even assist with bath time. Younger children can be taught to gently brush the Pug's back, staying away from the head and other sensitive areas. If the child is too young or unpredictable, thereby causing a potential danger to the Pug, let the child help by handing the grooming tools to the person performing the brushing.

best route to good dental health. To start, you'll need a dog toothbrush and dog toothpaste. Toothbrushes made for dogs may appear to be a smaller version of a human toothbrush, or they may have bristles at both ends. There is also a style of toothbrush that fits on your finger like a thimble for better control in a small mouth. When it comes to toothpaste, there is a variety of flavoured types available that many dogs find tasty. Only use toothpaste made specifically for dogs—never use human toothpaste as it could be toxic to your Pug.

Ideally, the Pug should be introduced to brushing the teeth at an early age. Start by letting him lick a small amount of dog toothpaste

off your finger, and gradually familiarise him with each step of the process. Brushing your Pug's teeth should be done daily, or at the very least, three times a week.

Brushing your Pug's teeth can be done on a grooming table, or some owners prefer to sit face-to-face with their Pug on a couch or on the floor. Only the outside of the teeth need to be brushed, and there is no need to rinse. Work on one side of the mouth at a time. Lift the dog's lip on one side and brush each tooth in a circular motion. Repeat on the other side.

If your Pug is like mine and clamps her jaws tighter than a rusty screw at the sight of a toothbrush, an alternative is to use a dental oral rinse with a thin nozzle that can be squirted into the mouth. An oral rinse is not as effective as brushing but will offer some protection.

Combined with brushing or an oral rinse, dental chew toys can assist in maintaining dental health. As with any chew or toy, you should supervise your Pug to keep him safe.

Your Pug may need a professional dental cleaning from your veterinarian if he has halitosis (bad breath), shows signs plaque build up, or you notice tooth loss or cracked or chipped teeth. Taking care of your Pug's teeth now can prevent further and more serious problems in the future.

Attire and Accessories

One of the pleasures of owning a Pug is that there is a cornucopia of dog clothes made for the toy breeds and

Grooming as a Health Check

While grooming your Pug, be on the look out for of any signs of a potential or existing health problem.

- Do his ears, nose roll, or mouth have a bad odour?
- Do his eyes look normal or is there excessive discharge, brown spots, or a blue cast to them?
- Do you feel any strange bumps that could be tumours or ticks?
- Does the flea comb indicate a flea infestation?
- Are his nails the proper length?
- Are the pads of his paws in good condition?
- Is he overly sensitive to your touch in an area that had never bothered him before?

It is important to be aware of any changes in your Pug's body as well as any changes in behaviour. If you suspect a problem, contact your veterinarian.

other small to medium dogs. Pet shops carry doggy T-shirts, sweaters, and dog coats. Holiday outfits and Halloween costumes are also available.

Doggy coats and sweaters can be both fun and functional in cold weather. However, do not dress your Pug in warm clothing if he could get overheated during an indoor event or an outside event on a warm or hot day. The same holds true for holiday costumes. If it is too warm for your Pug to be in costume, only put it on for the short time he may be entered in a costume contest or having his picture taken.

Always put safety first when choosing attire or accessories for your Pug. Make sure to measure him to get the correct size clothing—a Pug could trip or get tangled in a size that is too large. Clothing that is too small could injure the Pug and even restrict blood flow.

Looking Good

Some Pugs like to keep warm in the winter months with a sweater.

Chapter 5

Feeling Good

One of the primary responsibilities of pet ownership is keeping your pet healthy. Preventative care includes annual check-ups and a vaccination schedule. The annual check-up is a good way to catch a health concern early in order to reduce or eradicate a more serious problem that could develop over time. A veterinarian who is familiar with your Pug's medical history will have an advantage when diagnosing and treating him for any health concerns.

Every breed is predisposed to certain health issues. The Pug is prone to respiratory, eye, dental, hip, and skin disorders. Does that mean your Pug will acquire these problems? Not necessarily, but you need to be knowledgeable and vigilant about these potential issues. You also need to be aware of any changes to your Pug physically or with his behaviour that could indicate a health problem.

Finding the Right Vet

The veterinarian that you choose for your Pug should be both knowledgeable and experienced at treating brachycephalic (flat faced) breeds. Brachycephalic breeds are prone to specific respiratory issues that result from the structure of the head.

If you acquired your Pug locally, ask the breeder, shelter, or rescue organisation where you obtained your Pug to recommend a Pug-experienced veterinarian. Local pet supply stores may also have the scoop on local vets. Ask your dog-owning neighbours if they are satisfied with their veterinarian.

Whether a veterinarian was recommended or you had to resort to the phone book to locate one, check out the surgery prior to making an appointment for your Pug. Ask for a tour of the facilities. Inquire as to what medical or surgical services can be provided and the average cost for routine services. And most important of all, ask if the staff is experienced with

brachycephalic breeds.

Another important consideration is access to emergency care when the veterinarian's surgery is closed for the day. Few veterinarians offer a 24 hour emergency service though they may have a contingency plan for regular patients. Some surgeries may have a vet on call for emergencies but only during specified off hours. You may be referred to a veterinary teaching hospital's emergency room or an animal emergency centre if there is one located in your area. Make sure that you know how your

veterinarian handles

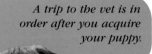

A trip to the vet is in order after you acquire your puppy.

emergencies in the off hours *before* you have the need for such a service.

Puppy's First Vet Visit

Part of the process of acquiring a new puppy is a trip to the veterinarian for an evaluation of the puppy's health condition. This should be done as soon as possible after welcoming your puppy home as some problems aren't obvious through mere observation. If the puppy is due for any of his vaccinations, they will be administered at that time, and the vet will discuss a vaccination schedule with you.

The vet will check the eyes, ears, coat, and listen to the heart and lungs. The vet will also look for any joint problems such as in the knees (luxating patella) and hips (hip dysplasia). You may be asked to bring a stool sample to the visit which will be tested for worms and other potential problems.

Hopefully, puppy's first vet visit will be just a wellness check, but if any current or potential problems arise, the vet can advise a course of action.

Annual Vet Visit

Our pets can't tell us when they aren't feeling well or are in pain. While some dogs can indicate problems by their behaviour, the Pug is a stoic breed, which makes it even more difficult to determine if there is a problem.

That's why the annual vet visit is an important part of keeping your Pug healthy. It gives your vet the chance to identify any potential or existing problems and to discuss possible

FAMILY-FRIENDLY TIP

Your Child and the Vet

If your child is uncomfortable going to the doctor's surgery, he or she will probably be uncomfortable accompanying you and your pet to the veterinarian. Explain what to expect in both the waiting area and treatment room in terms appropriate to the age of the child. If your child is young or very sensitive, bring another adult along who can supervise the child or take him or her out to the waiting area if need be. A routine veterinary visit is a better choice than an emergency visit to acclimate your child to responsible pet health care.

treatment plans with you. If a health issue arises in the future, your vet can compare your Pug's previous health records with any new findings.

Advances in veterinary medicine combined with more attention paid to the various life stages of the dog means our pets are living longer. Some veterinarians now offer programmes from puppy wellness to senior care. Puppies, seniors, and dogs with specific medical issues may need more frequent follow-ups than one annual exam, but a

Feeling Good

yearly vet visit should suffice for a healthy adult.

Vaccinations

As of this writing, the subject of vaccinations is a controversial topic. There are core vaccinations all dogs need, but the safety and/or effectiveness of certain vaccines is being questioned; and some vaccines have a significant risk factor for small dogs. The need to give your pet vaccinations every year is also being debated, because some vaccines provide years of protection. The major concern among vets and health experts is that dogs are being over-vaccinated.

Deciding which vaccinations your Pug should receive, as well as how often, can be very confusing for a pet owner. Opinions vary among veterinarians and even among Pug breeders.

If you purchased your Pug from a reputable breeder, he or she can advise you as to what vaccinations your Pug may need and whether or not their Pugs have a history of a bad reaction to certain vaccines.

Another important factor to consider is the prevalence of specific canine diseases where you live. Be aware that a vaccine for a disease may not be effective if does not target the specific strain of the disease that your dog could be exposed to. Talk to veterinarians, Pug breeders, Pug owners, and dog experts to gather information. The bottom line is that *you* must be the advocate for your Pug.

Two of the vaccines that are of concern to owners of small dogs, including the Pug, are the leptospirosis vaccine and the corona virus vaccine. Both may cause an allergic reaction that can vary from very mild to deadly.

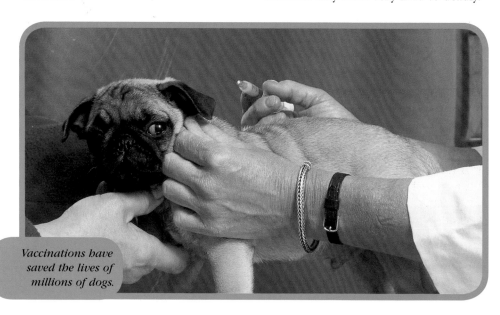

Vaccinations have saved the lives of millions of dogs.

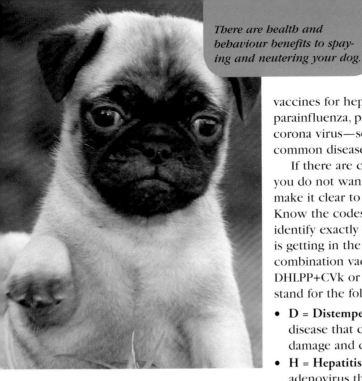

against distemper, it may also include the vaccines for hepatitis, leptospirosis, parainfluenza, parvovirus, and corona virus—some of the most common diseases that affect dogs.

If there are certain vaccines that you do not want your Pug to have, make it clear to your veterinarian. Know the codes so that you can identify exactly what your Pug is getting in the vaccine. The combination vaccine may be labeled DHLPP+CVk or DA2PPV. The letters stand for the following diseases:

- **D = Distemper:** a viral infectious disease that causes neurological damage and can be fatal.
- **H = Hepatitis:** caused by an adenovirus that attacks the liver and can be fatal.
- **A2 = Adenovirus type 2** (also known as hepatitis); also attacks the liver
- **L = Leptospirosis:** a bacterial infection that damages the liver and kidneys and can be fatal. Many puppies and toy breeds have allergic reactions to this vaccine which range in severity from mild to fatal.
- **P = Parainfluenza:** a disease that can affect the stomach, bone marrow, and lymph nodes.
- **P or PV = Parvovirus:** a virus that affects the intestinal tract and can be fatal.
- **CVk = Corona virus (killed):** a virus that may attack the respiratory or gastrointestinal systems. It can be fatal, but less

On the other side of the coin, the danger of the diseases themselves can also be mild to fatal for dogs. Adding to the confusion is that a new strain of leptospirosis has been identified, which isn't covered by current vaccines. The questions to ask your vet about any vaccine are, "Is this vaccine targeting the current strain of the disease?" and "How safe it is for the Pug breed and other small breeds?"

What to Vaccinate Against

Your vet will most likely recommend a "distemper" shot for your Pug. It is vital for pet owners to understand that what your veterinarian refers to as the distemper shot is most likely a combination distemper vaccine. This means that in addition to vaccinating

55

Feeling Good

severe reactions are more common.

In addition to these seven diseases found in the combination vaccination, your Pug may need the following vaccinations:

- **Rabies:** a highly contagious and deadly disease that affects the brain. Necessary if travelling abroad with your Pug.
- **Bordatella:** a highly contagious airborne respiratory

If your Pug's ears appear red, have him checked out by his vet.

disease. It is also known as kennel cough, because it is easily transmitted among dogs sharing space, such as in a kennel.

- **Lyme disease:** a disease transmitted by a tick; causes severe arthritis. Usually only recommended if Lyme disease is prevalent in your area. Tick preventatives are available if you prefer not to vaccinate.

Pet Insurance

Pet insurance is now available and accepted at many veterinary surgeries. Before signing up for pet insurance, compare rates and what treatments are included and excluded from coverage. Some insurance companies do not cover illnesses that are commonly associated with a particular breed. Also, a pre-existing condition may not be covered. To determine if it is worth obtaining pet insurance, compare the cost of the insurance plan with your usual veterinary expenses. You should also consider how you would cover an unexpected and costly treatment or surgery.

Neutering and Spaying

Pet owners should have their male dogs neutered and female dogs spayed to avoid the proliferation of unwanted or unhealthy puppies. Show dogs must remain unaltered to qualify for the show ring, specifically in conformation. Dogs who do not qualify for the show ring are referred to as "pet quality." They are usually perfectly healthy and wonderful dogs who for whatever reason do not meet the breed standard. A responsible and reputable breeder will either have her pet quality dogs neutered or spayed prior to selling them, or will have the new owner sign a contract agreeing to have the dog altered. It is not advisable for a pet owner to breed a small dog like the Pug as the pregnancy and delivery have a greater chance of complications. The need for a caesarean section for a small dog is not uncommon.

Although it may be obvious to spay your female Pug to avoid an unwanted pregnancy, it is equally important to have your male Pug neutered, even if he is the only dog in your household. There is always the possibility he could get loose and enjoy a tryst with a neighbourhood cutie. Plus, anywhere he goes where there are other dogs, such as parks, playgroups, and training classes, your bachelor Pug will be scouting out the ladies (most likely annoying them) and will take advantage of any unsupervised moment.

There are also health and behaviour benefits to spaying and neutering your dog. Females will be less likely to develop mammary gland tumours; males will be less likely to mark their territory with urine and be less aggressive toward other male dogs.

Potential Pug Illnesses and Conditions

Every breed is vulnerable to certain hereditary illnesses or conditions that can lead to a medical problem, and the Pug is no exception. Also, keep in mind that this breed's propensity towards obesity can significantly aggravate any medical condition.

Diabetes

The overweight Pug is at risk for developing diabetes. In fact, the Pug rescue organisation to which I belong has seen an increase in obese Pugs with this disease. Diabetes is a disease in which the pancreas cannot manufacture insulin or produce it in sufficient amounts. Insulin is a hormone that converts sugar (glucose), starches, and other foods into energy, and moves it from the blood into the cells. Without adequate insulin, the glucose

The shortness of the Pug's nose and face increases the potential for breathing difficulties.

cannot enter the cells and provide energy that the cells require. The resulting glucose build up will cause high-blood sugar. High-blood sugar can lead to a number of medical conditions such as heart disease, kidney disease, nerve damage, and blindness. Treatment for diabetes includes daily insulin injections.

Ear Conditions

If your Pug's ears have a bad odour or appear red, he has an ear infection. Symptoms also include shaking his head, scratching at one or both ears, or dragging his ear on the floor.

Otitis Externa

This is a common ear infection that can result in inflammation of the outer ear. Otitis externa may be caused by a mite infestation, excess wax. or a build up of debris. A veterinarian can prescribe the proper ear cleaner to rid the ear of infection.

Eye Conditions

Since the Pug is genetically predisposed to certain eye diseases, a reputable breeder will have his or her Pug's eyes certified clear of problems by the British Veterinary Association, prior to using that Pug in a breeding programme.

The Pug's large globular eyes are particularly vulnerable to injury. If your Pug sustains a serious eye injury or develops an eye disease, ask your vet to recommend a veterinary ophthalmologist.

The following eye diseases are common to the Pug breed.

Entropion

In this condition, the eyelid rolls under toward the eye and the hair rubs against the eyeball. Without treatment, the eye can be damaged. Surgery can correct this problem.

Keratoconjunctivitis Sicca (KCS)

KCS is also known as "dry eye," because Pugs with this condition are unable to produce the normal tear secretions required to protect the eye. If left untreated, the Pug is vulnerable to eye abrasions. Treatment may include daily eye drops to lubricate the eyes.

Pigmentary Keratitus (PK)

PK is inflammation of the cornea. Dark spots manifest on the surface of the eye, usually in the corner closest to the nose. As the spots spread across the cornea, the Pug will lose his sight. It is imperative to begin treatment as soon as possible to avoid further damage to the eye. Treatment may include eye drops that in some cases may remove or retard the spread of the pigment. Surgery may be needed to remove the pigmented layers.

Trichiasis

This condition is caused by the Pug's own facial hair or eyelashes rubbing against the eye. The nose fold raises the hairs close to eye level, and the friction of the hair against the eye causes eye inflammation. This is treated by the surgical removal of the hairs.

Heatstroke

Dogs do not sweat—they release body heat through the respiratory system by panting. Brachycephalic (flat-faced) breeds, including the Pug, have a less efficient respiratory system due to the head structure. Since it is more difficult to release heat through the respiratory system, these breeds are prone to succumbing to heat. Rapid panting signals that this process is being overtaxed.

Heatstroke is a dangerous and life-threatening condition. Causes of heat stroke include prolonged exposure to the hot sun or being kept in enclosed areas with high temperatures or poor ventilation. Leaving a dog in a car on a warm or hot day is one way to cause a dangerous case of heatstroke. Even on a mild day with the windows partially open, the temperature can rise rapidly, and the end result can be fatal.

Symptoms of heatstroke include:
- Heavy panting
- Rapid breathing
- Bright red tongue
- Gums becoming red, then progressing to white and/or blue
- Loss of balance
- Weakness
- Vomiting
- Uncontrollable urinating or diarrhoea
- Shock
- Coma

The following tips will help to cool the dog down until you can get to a veterinarian:

- Apply rubbing alcohol to the dog's paw pads.
- Apply ice packs to the groin area.
- Hose down the dog with water.
- Allow the dog to lick ice chips or drink a small amount of water.
- Offer rehydration fluids to restore electrolytes.

Feeling Good

Neurological Disorders

The following are potential neurological disorders found in Pugs.

Idiopathic Epilepsy

Epilepsy is a neurological disease that causes seizures. If the cause of the epilepsy is unknown, it is referred to as idiopathic. Although epilepsy can be controlled with medication, there is no cure.

Pug Dog Encephalitis (PDE)

PDE is an inflammation of the brain and the surrounding membranes, which also connect to the nerves and the spinal cord. This disease only affects the Pug breed. There is no known cause, no cure, and it is always fatal (though some treatments may extend the Pug's life for several months). PDE is usually seen in young Pugs under two-years of age. Symptoms include seizures, circling, pressing the head against a hard surface, staggering, and blindness. Scientific research is currently being conducted on PDE in an effort to understand this baffling disease.

Orthopaedic Conditions

Like certain eye disorders, the Pug is also genetically prone to certain orthopaedic disorders. The Kennel Club and British Veterinary Association (BVA) run a programme offering breeders tests for potential problems.

Any Pug who is not cleared of a defect or potential disorder is not bred, thereby preventing his or her puppies from inheriting and passing on a genetic defect.

The following are potential orthopaedic problems your Pug may face.

Hip Dysplasia

Hip dysplasia is dislocation of the hip. This can be a very painful and crippling disease. Normally, the head of the femur fits snugly into the hip socket. If the femur doesn't fit correctly, the slippage and friction will damage the cartilage and result in joint inflammation. This will eventually lead to arthritis.

A glucosamine supplement may help a dog in the early stages of this disease. Glucosamine production is what keeps the connective tissue and joints lubricated and elastic for ease of movement. Surgery may be necessary in severe cases.

Legg-Calve-Perthes Disease

This degenerative disease affects many of the toy breeds. Due to insufficient blood supply, the femur (thighbone) deteriorates, which results in lameness. This disease usually appears within the first ten months

First Aid Kit

Keeping a first-aid kit on hand will enable you to take care of minor medical emergencies. In the event of a serious medical situation that requires a trip to the veterinarian or an animal hospital, time is often of the essence. A first-aid kit could play an important role in buying time while getting your Pug to a veterinarian.

First-aid kits can be purchased ready-made, or you can make your own. Keep medicines in a cool, dry place. Items to have on hand include:

- Gauze pads and rolls
- Adhesive tape
- Scissors
- Tweezers
- Cotton balls and swabs
- Gloves
- Thermometer—rectal or digital (Normal temperature range: 100 to 102°F [37.7 to 38.8°C])
- Syringe for oral medication
- Topical antibiotic solution, for cleaning wounds
- Styptic powder to stop minor cuts
- Saline solution to rinse the eyes
- Hydrogen peroxide to clean wounds. Also used to induce vomiting. (Caution: amount and frequency determined by dog's weight—ask your vet for the ratio)
- Cotton balls and swabs
- Aspirin for pain (Caution: do not use other pain relievers such as Ibuprofen, which are poisonous to dogs.)
- Pepto Bismol or Immodium for diarrhoea
- Benadryl anti-histamine for allergic reactions

Some Pugs have nostrils that are too tiny, which causes breathing problems.

Collapsing Trachea

The trachea (windpipe) may become too soft as a result of ageing or obesity. A soft trachea can collapse from either internal or external pressure. Internal pressure may result when an overexcited Pug suddenly increases his intake of air through heavy panting or barking. External pressure comes from the outside, such as a dog collar pressing on the throat. To prevent this condition, a Pug with a soft trachea should wear a harness instead of a collar.

Elongated Soft Palate

An elongated soft palate is a problem also associated with brachycephalic breeds. The soft palate is the flap of skin at the back of the throat. If the palate is too long, it can prevent sufficient air from getting into the lungs, which makes it harder for the Pug to breathe. He may snort or gasp in an attempt to get more air. An elongated soft palate puts the Pug at risk for heart and lung complications; he could also collapse from lack of oxygen. This condition can be corrected with surgery.

of the Pug's life. Surgery is needed to repair this condition.

Luxating Patella

The patella is the kneecap; luxation is the dislocation of a joint. A luxating patella is dislocation of the knee. The patella is normally held in a socket in the femur (thighbone) by ligaments. In mild cases, the patella may pop out and then return to its normal position. In severe cases, the patella is not able to stay in place and will need to be corrected with surgery.

Respiratory Conditions

The Pug is a brachycephalic breed, and this shortness of the nose and face increases the potential for breathing difficulties.

Stenotic Nares

Stenotic nares are narrow or very tiny nostrils. When the nasal passage is restricted, the Pug has trouble breathing out of his nose, and will resort to breathing out of his mouth—a much less efficient way of breathing. It also puts undue strain on the heart and could lead to heart failure. Stenotic nares can be corrected with surgery.

Skin Conditions

If your Pug is scratching at his skin, or biting or licking it excessively, this indicates he has a skin condition which needs to be addressed. Red or bald patches are symptoms of a more serious condition.

Acne

Just like human adolescents, the adolescent Pug is prone to acne. Pimples on the face may appear between six-months and two-years of age. If your Pug has acne, keep his face clean and do not squeeze the pimples. If the area becomes infected, his vet may prescribe an antibiotic. If the acne is caused by irritating hairs beneath the surface, the vet may prescribe an anti-inflammatory medicine.

Allergic Dermatitis

The Pug is susceptible to allergies. In addition to scratching, biting and licking the skin, he may exhibit

sneezing and snuffling (a reverse sneeze). It may take some experimentation to figure out if the root cause is an allergic reaction to a food, an inhalant such as pollen or dust, or another environmental factor. Some Pugs have an allergic reaction to flea saliva, which is secreted into the skin as the flea feeds. Be aware that some Pugs have a combination of allergies.

There is a variety of treatments for allergies, and it may take you and your veterinarian a few tries to find the one that works best for your Pug. If the allergen is identified, the easiest step (if possible) is avoidance. Topical treatments or hypoallergenic shampoos may relieve itching. Dietary supplements that contain biotin or essential fatty acids such as omega-3 can reduce allergic reactions in some dogs. Antihistimine treatment is another option. Glucorticoids are

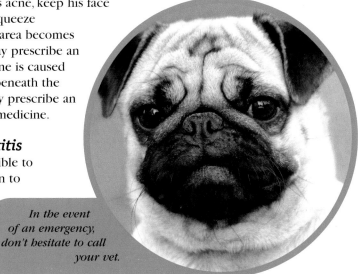

In the event of an emergency, don't hesitate to call your vet.

prescribed in severe cases, but steroids are not recommended for long term use. Another option for severe cases is immunotherapy, which involves a skin test to determine the offending allergen(s), and then desensitising the dog by a series of injections containing a small amount of the allergen.

Demodectic Mange

Demodectic mange (sometimes called demodex) is caused by an excessive infestation of demodex mites. While a low number of demodex mites is normal on a healthy dog, if the number of mites becomes excessive, demodex mange can result. Often, a Pug may pass demodex mites onto her puppies during close contact—the reason why this condition is usually seen in younger Pugs rather than mature Pugs. An infected area will be bald and red and will need to be treated by a veterinarian.

General Illnesses and Problems

There are other illnesses that are not breed-specific that dogs sometimes face. Annual vet visits, a good diet, and attention to your Pug's overall health can help avoid problems before they start.

Anal Glands

Dogs have two anal or scent glands, one located on each side of the rectum. The anal glands contain a malodourous substance and empty

when the dog defecates. At least that is what is supposed to happen.

If your Pug is scooting across the floor on his rear end, his anal glands are full and need to be emptied because the glands did not empty naturally. Anal glands that are not emptied may become impacted and push out through the dog's skin creating a lesion.

There are two methods of manually expressing the anal glands. One is external, which can often be done by a groomer, and the other is internal, which is done by a veterinarian or vet technician.

Cancer

Dogs of any breed can get cancer—most who do will develop it in their senior years. Early detection and treatment is crucial. Be aware of any lumps that form on your Pug, unusual swelling, wounds

Mange is usually seen only in puppies.

Check your Pug for fleas and ticks after he's been outside.

that do not heal, or loss of interest in food or activity.

Fleas and Ticks

Fleas can be the bane of a dog owner's existence if precautions are not taken to ward off an infestation. Chapter 4 explained how to check for fleas with a comb, but prevention is really the best way to deal with this problem. Ask your veterinarian to recommend a safe flea prevention product for your Pug, as well as a product for ridding a flea problem. When my Pug was a puppy, she was overly sensitive to anything that could cause an allergic reaction. My veterinarian suggested that we try a natural flea preventative rather than a chemical treatment. I put her on brewer's yeast and garlic tablets, which also contain omega-3 fatty acids. She

has been receiving his treatment for over eight years, and she has never had fleas. While this natural treatment may not work for every dog, it may be worth a try.

The tick is a parasite that feeds on the blood of people and animals and can cause serious illnesses, such as Lyme disease. Be sure to check your Pug for ticks after he has been outside. Ticks prefer the head, neck, ears, feet, and underbelly or any area that is easy for them to latch on.

If you find a tick on your Pug, carefully remove it with tweezers. Get hold of the tick as closely as you can to the dog's skin, then pull up slowly. Dispose of the tick by dropping it into a container of rubbing alcohol.

You can find a preventative that combines protections against both fleas and ticks. Even if you use a preventative, always check your Pug for ticks after he has been outside.

Poisoning

There are many items in the home that are poisonous to dogs. Human medications, household cleaning products, anti-freeze, mothballs—the list goes on and on.

If your Pug ingests a toxic substance, call your veterinarian immediately to prewarn of your imminent arrival.

Toxic Foods

Toxic foods ingested by your Pug may cause reactions that can range from mild to fatal. Smaller dogs like the Pug are more susceptible to having a severe or fatal reaction. A partial list of toxic foods includes:

- alcoholic drinks
- apple seeds
- caffeinated drinks such as coffee
- chocolate
- grapes and raisins
- macadamia nuts
- mushrooms
- onions
- peach leaves and stones
- potato (all green parts)
- tomato plant (except ripe fruit)
- Xylitol (an artificial sweetener in foods).

Toxic Flowers and Plants

While some dogs may be content to just stop and smell the roses and other flowers, others prefer to taste test anything in their path. This is especially true of puppies who are learning about their surroundings. It is important to be aware that certain flowers and plants are toxic to dogs. See the box "Plants and Flowers Toxic to Your Pug" for some of the more common toxic flowers and plants.

Urinary Conditions

A Pug who is urinating frequently, has trouble urinating, or has blood droplets in his urine will need a urine test performed by a veterinarian to determine the cause. If a Pug is having potty accidents in the house it could be due to a urinary problem.

Urinary Tract Infections (UTI)

A UTI is a bacterial infection. Left untreated, it can lead to kidney failure. Pugs with UTI may have difficultly or pain when urinating,

Check your garden for potentially harmful plants and flowers.

Plants and Flowers Toxic to Your Pug

The following is just a partial list of toxic flowers and plants:

- aloe vera
- asparagus fern
- azalea
- begonia
- carnation
- chives
- chrysanthemum
- clematis
- corn plant
- crocus
- daffodil
- eucalyptus
- foxglove
- gladiola
- hemlock
- hyacinth
- hydrangea
- iris
- ivy
- jonquil
- lily
- lupine
- marigold
- milkweed
- morning glory
- narcissus
- nightshade
- philodendron
- poppy
- rhododendron
- rhubarb
- shamrock plant
- toadstools
- tobacco
- tulip
- wisteria

or they may be urinating too frequently. Other symptoms include fever and lethargy.

A UTI is treated with antibiotics.

Urinary Calculi or Stones

A urinary tract infection may be accompanied by calculi (stones), which will need to be surgically removed. If caught early, the urine may contain crystals which have not yet formed into stones. In this case, treatment will include medication along with flushing out the crystals by getting more fluid into the Pug.

Holistic/Alternative Therapies

The word holistic refers to treating "the whole." Holistic medicine (sometimes called "alternative") takes into account the patient's mind, body, and spirit. Alternative therapies are used to promote wellness and treat the whole patient, rather than just treating a specific symptom like conventional medicine. Alternative therapies also tend to be less invasive than conventional treatments. These therapies are often used in conjunction with conventional care. Always have your Pug evaluated by a qualified veterinarian and discuss the appropriateness of specific alternative therapies.

Alternative therapies are available through holistic veterinarians, and some conventional veterinarians may offer one or more of these services.

Alternative therapies include:

- **Acupuncture**: removes blockages to the patient's vital force (Chi) by inserting needles into acupuncture points that correspond to the part of the body that needs healing.

- **Chiropractic**: identifies and corrects subluxations (misalignments) in the

Feeling Good

spine by making manual adjustments.

- **Homeopathy**: based on the theory "like cures like"; a specific substance (e.g., plant, animal, mineral, bacteria) with properties associated with an illness or disorder is administered in minute amounts, whereas the same substance could be toxic in large amounts.
- **Chinese herbs**: herbalists in the Chinese tradition prepare customised blends that are used to promote the balance of the yin and yang (opposite manifestations in nature) for the purpose of maintaining well-being and vitality, or to bring an ill body back into balance.
- **Western herbs**: the Western (or European) method traditionally uses a single herb source that corresponds to a specific need, rather than a blend of herbs that is common in the Chinese tradition.
- **Nutritional therapy**: a customised diet using preservative-free, healthy foods.
- **Bach flowers**: flower essences in liquid form administered by placing a few drops on the tongue or in drinking water for the purpose of eliminating disharmony and emotional imbalance that contribute to illness. "Rescue Remedy," a combination of flower essences, is used to counteract stress or trauma caused by a crisis.
- **Massage therapy**: massaging the muscles to reduce stress, or to manage or relieve pain.

- **Magnetic therapy**: a magnet is placed on the problem area allowing the magnetic field to enhance the body's natural healing ability and is frequently used to reduce or relieve pain, improve circulation, and restore energy.
- **Reiki**: a Japanese healing and stress reduction technique in which the practitioner draws upon universal life energy (Chi), and through his or her hands, redirects the flow to unblock the patient's Chi.

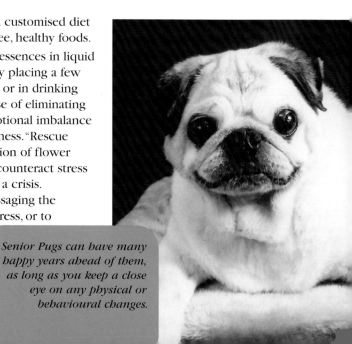

Senior Pugs can have many happy years ahead of them, as long as you keep a close eye on any physical or behavioural changes.

SENIOR DOG TIP
Senior Pugs

The Pug enters his senior years around the age of eight, but chances are he still has many happy years ahead of him. Pugs have been known to surpass the age of 15. Although the Pug is prone to more health issues in his senior years, his personality and devotion will more than make up for it.

The senior Pug should be observed more closely by his owner for any changes in behaviour that may indicate a health problem. Just like people, the older Pug may have decreased hearing and eyesight, need more frequent bathroom breaks, have a more sensitive digestive system, and feel more achy and tired. Now that dogs live longer—thanks to better care and diet—illnesses such cancer and heart disease are popping up in the senior population.

Some veterinarians offer a senior programme which includes blood tests and X-rays to determine the dog's state of health. The purpose of senior testing is to uncover any possible problems that are in the early stage, or to have a baseline for comparison purposes in the event of an illness.

As for day to day living with a senior Pug, bear in mind that his energy level may be lower and to adjust his walks and exercise accordingly. As his metabolism slows down, his diet should be adjusted so that he does not become obese. He may have medications that need to be given daily. If the energy of younger dogs or children annoys him when he needs to rest, make sure he has his own quiet space.

On the plus side, the senior is a "professional Pug"—he's had a lifetime of perfecting his companionship duties and comedic skills. Although he may be a little slower in the physical department, his love will continue to warm your heart and your lap.

Chapter 6

Being Good

What if I told you that there is a magical language that would allow you to communicate clearly with your Pug? Wouldn't it be time or money well spent to learn how to "talk" to your little Pug like Dr. Doolittle? Well, such a language does indeed exist, and it is easy to learn with a little practice. It's called dog training. What's so magical about that? Consider the person with a chronically misbehaving dog who continually ignores his owner's instructions. When that person observes someone else who can control his or her dog with a few words or hand signals, it must seem like magic. But the real magic is that we all can communicate with our Pugs—we just need to learn how.

Training your Pug is the most worthwhile activity that you can share with him. A well-trained Pug will guarantee years of happiness for both Pug and owner. The number one reason that dogs end up in shelters or in rescue is lack of training.

Yes, training takes time and consistency on your part, but doesn't it make more sense to spend a few hours a week training him to be well-behaved than spending time cleaning up a mess or trying to stop unwanted behaviour?

Start Training Early

Begin teaching basic commands when your Pug joins the family, but remember to be patient as he is also adjusting to a new environment. Whether he is a puppy, an adult, or a senior, he needs to learn the house rules.

A young puppy will take longer to learn the rules. He is still a new being in the world, so every day is an adventure, his attention span is short, and he will have spurts of high energy between his naps. Extra patience is also needed with the senior Pug who may not be able to move as fast when you give a command, or he may have hearing or vision problems.

The Pug responds best to rewards and praise and will do his best to please you. This desire to please is an important element in training your Pug. Be patient and have fun. If you act like training is chore, your Pug will pick up on it and not want to work either. If he feels

The Pug is a breed who enjoys the company of children.

pressured or forced to do something, he'll display the infamous Pug stubborn streak and nothing will get accomplished.

A positive attitude and the repetition of training techniques will shape your Pug into a well-behaved dog. Consistency in training is imperative, whether it's teaching your dog to walk on his lead or housetraining. Make sure that all family members are using the same commands to train your Pug. Make sure, too, that all family members understand and enforce the rules. If you've decided that there is a "no feeding from the dinner table" rule everyone must follow through with it. Your Pug will not understand that sometimes it's okay (when it's "just the family") and sometimes it's not (when the boss is over for dinner).

Don't blame your Pug for misbehaving if you haven't taught him properly. It's up to you to become a good leader and enforce the rules. This doesn't mean screaming and yelling—it means spending time positively training your Pug so he can be a well-behaved and fun member of the family.

Socialisation

Socialisation is the act of making a dog comfortable in various situations by exposing him to a variety of people, other pets, and unfamiliar environments. These new experiences should be pleasant and safe. It is critical that the socialisation process begin when the dog is a puppy and still under the breeder's care. Puppies learn to socialise with their own kind while with their dam (mother) and their littermates. The breeder and his or her family provide the initial exposure to humans.

Dogs who are not properly socialised may exhibit anxiety or shyness around new people or animals. When an unsocialised dog feels threatened, he may cower or develop fear-related aggression. Most Pugs crave human attention so it is hard to imagine a Pug who avoids it or fears it. Unfortunately, it does happen as a result of poor breeding, lack of socialisation, or abuse. Sometimes a Pug coming from these circumstances can be rehabilitated if he is paired with the right person who has the love and patience

to work with him.

Taking a class with other people and their dogs helps socialise your Pug—and it's fun. Classes may be available through a local pet shop or at a veterinarian's surgery. Most sites offer a variety of classes to accommodate different ages and levels of training.

Puppy kindergarten provides socialisation with other puppies and people and introduces the puppy to the basic commands. Puppy issues such as housetraining are also addressed. Instructors usually require that puppies fall within a certain age group (e.g., puppies must be at least three-months-old but less than six-months-old.)

A young puppy will take longer to learn the rules.

Beginning Obedience classes usually have a minimum age requirement such as six-months-old, but dogs of any age older than that may take the class. This type of class teaches the basic commands and how to train your dog to have good manners. Intermediate Obedience classes can serve as a refresher course for you and your dog and as an opportunity to work on any commands that are problematic.

FAMILY-FRIENDLY TIP

Bringing Home Baby

Many Pugs end up in rescue or a shelter when their owners bring home a new baby. By preparing ahead, this sad option can be avoided. To acclimate your Pug to the coming change in his daily routine, implement the new routine a few weeks before the baby's expected arrival. Before the day you bring baby home from the hospital, take home an item with the baby's scent on it, such as a blanket or the little hat worn in the hospital and give it to your Pug. Now when baby arrives home, his or her scent will be familiar to your Pug, which will help him be more accepting of the new family member.

With Children

The Pug is a breed who enjoys the company of children, and his appearance and personality draw children to him. That being said, extra care should be taken when socialising a dog to children. For the safety of all, it is important to instil in both dog and child what is appropriate behaviour when spending time together. An adult should always monitor each session when the dog and child interact, until both parties have proven themselves trustworthy. Babies and very young children should always be monitored around pets. With older children, the age and maturity of both the dog and the child will factor into the socialisation process.

Is your Pug a puppy, adult, or senior? Puppies can be rambunctious. Playful nipping with littermates is normal but not a desired action with children. Older children can be involved in the process of discouraging nipping by giving a firm command such as "No bite." Younger children may panic or lash out thereby setting the stage for injury to either party. An adult or senior Pug needs to be evaluated for any health issues such as arthritis, which could be aggravated by the rough touch of a child.

Children must understand that caution needs to be taken around the Pug's eyes, which are prone to injury. Younger children tend to forget the rules, and they also lack physical coordination. Whether intentional or not, objects thrown to the Pug may hit him in the face and injure the eyes.

Being Good

must *never* hit, kick, or beat an animal. The Pug is not a breed that typically bites, but any dog that feels threatened may defend itself. Once both Pug and the child have learned how to properly interact, the stage is set for a priceless bonding experience.

If you have other household pets, you will need to socialise them to your new Pug.

Children must be taught that a dog is not a toy but a living being. Disciplining a dog must be in the form of a firm vocal command; they

With Other Pets

If you have other household pets, you will need to socialise them to your new Pug. If your pet is another dog (even if he is a Pug, too), have them meet for the first time on neutral territory. If your new Pug is coming from a breeder, shelter, or rescue organisation, ask if you can take your dog to meet the Pug at that location. If that's not possible, the dogs could meet outside on the pavement, sniff and greet, then head into the house.

Once home, always monitor the interaction between your new Pug and other pets until you are confident that they will get along. Anytime you cannot monitor them, place the Pug in his crate or other safe environment.

If your other pet is a dog, reassure him that he has not lost his status as number one dog in the household. At mealtimes and snack times, feed him first. If you have more than one dog, feed each dog in the order that they came into your household. Dogs are pack animals, and by preserving the

status quo, you can eliminate the need for territorial challenges.

If your other pet is cat, take into consideration your cat's personality. If your cat has never been around dogs, you will have to closely monitor her behaviour, which may be unpredictable with the new family member. Pugs usually get along with cats, but make sure the feeling is mutual to avoid injury to either pet. Use the same caution when introducing your new Pug to pets of other species.

Crate Training

I still remember the first time I heard someone mention that she put her dog in a crate. I was horrified, imagining the poor dog being caged inside a makeshift jail. This assumption could not have been more wrong, as I learned later when preparing for the arrival of my new Pug puppy. Crates are a good thing. The crate is a valuable

A crate provides your Pug with his own personal space.

tool for the dog owner and a safe haven for the dog.

In retrospect, it was the word *crate* that gave me pause. Crates are containers that you pack things in, like eggs. If dog crates had been called "mobile doggy dens," I probably wouldn't have rushed to judgement and deemed crates as cruel.

In reality, a dog crate serves a noble purpose. It provides a dog his own personal space—his own room within the home. The crate recreates the wolf den of our dogs' ancestors. The wolf den provided shelter from the elements and was a hide-a-way from danger. In the safety and comfort of its den, the wolf could sleep, rest, and the females had a place to birth their wolf pups. Even in these modern times the dog, including the "unwolfy"-looking Pug, needs his own den—a quiet place to rest or sleep, away from the hubbub of family activity.

How to Crate Train

Begin by putting your Pug in the crate for short periods of time with the door open. Leaving favourite toys or treats inside, and even feeding your Pug in the crate will help create positive associations. Then put your Pug in the crate for short periods with the door closed and slowly begin to increase the time he's inside. Once your Pug has adjusted to the crate and no longer needs supervision, the crate door can be left open so that he can go in and out. This gives him his own indoor doghouse or personal space.

Overpampering

For the owner of a toy breed, it's not easy to resist overpampering your precious furry "child." Although the Pug is the largest of the toy breeds, he lives to be cuddled and coddled. Those big brown eyes can melt your heart to the point where you acquiesce to his every need. Of course, he deserves a little spoiling, but balance is the key. He needs to know that you are the leader, and you stand firm on any decisions regarding what he can or cannot have or do. An overpampered dog can become a tyrant and learn to control you, rather than the other way around. And that won't be a happy household.

When to Use the Crate

Remember, this is your Pug's place for pleasurable activities—eating, napping and relaxing—but no dog should be constantly confined in a crate. If your Pug is a puppy, new to your home, or needs supervision, the crate offers a safe place to put your Pug while you are out. But bear in mind that puppies cannot be crated for long periods of time, as they need to relieve themselves more frequently than adult dogs. Puppies should not be crated more than a few hours at a time. No dog, regardless of age, should be confined to a crate more than four hours at a time during the day.

Outdoor potty training takes patience and consistency.

A crate can be a valuable tool when a dog is recuperating from an illness or surgery and needs to stay quiet. There may also be times when it is in your dog's best interest to be crated, especially when being underfoot would be dangerous. Crating your Pug is also a good way to protect him from another pet or exuberant child if there is a potential for injury.

The crate can also be used for behaviour modification. For instance, if your dog won't stop barking, is being destructive, or getting into unacceptable mischief, try giving him a time out in the crate. However, being crated should not be viewed by the Pug as punishment. Let him have a chew toy to occupy his time in the crate.

Always remember to use the crate wisely and not confine your Pug for overextended periods of time. The crate is a tool to make life more pleasant for both dog and owner.

Housetraining

A stubborn or overpampered Pug may be harder to train if he knows he will get his way in the end. Housetraining is not an area where you want your Pug to call the shots. However, housetraining a Pug does not need to be difficult. The Pug responds well to calm, patient, and consistent training.

The crate is an important tool for housetraining your Pug. Dogs do not want to relieve themselves near where they eat and sleep, so if your Pug has accepted his crate as his "den," he won't want to go to the bathroom in it or near it. That is why the size of the crate matters—if it's too large, the dog may use the opposite end from the eating area as a bathroom.

Before you housetrain your Pug, decide *where* you want him to relieve himself: outside in a designated area or paper-trained indoors. Though some canine resources advocate choosing one or the other, my Pug is trained to go either outside or in my bathroom on a puppy pad secured in a tray. This comes in very handy during our New England winters, though most Pug owners here do train their Pugs to go outside exclusively.

Outdoor Training

Most puppies start out paper-trained and need to be taught to relieve themselves outside. An adult Pug who is trained to go outside will still need to learn where in the garden he is allowed to relieve himself. Dogs usually need to relieve themselves first thing in the morning, after a meal, and after an exuberant play session, exercise, or a walk. Puppies need more frequent potty breaks as they are unable to hold it for long periods of time.

Use small healthy treats to train your Pug.

Take your Pug to the designated area and say, "Go potty" or another phrase, such as "Hurry up." If your paper-trained puppy doesn't understand what you want him to do, place a piece of his pre-soiled paper on the grass where you want him to relieve himself. Praise him when he does his duty. By being patient, consistent, and using praise, your Pug will learn that this is his potty area.

Indoor Training

One of the benefits of owning a toy breed is that they can also be trained to go potty indoors. This is a convenient alternative for city dwellers in high-rises, the elderly or disabled, and folks who live in areas with extreme weather. Apply the same training technique as for outdoor potty training. Lead him to his potty area, say your phrase that means, "Go Potty," and praise him when he relieves himself. If he is confused, the next time he urinates, whether inside or outdoors, dip a small part of a clean puppy pad into his urine and place it in his new potty area. His scent on the pad will clarify what is expected of him.

While newspaper, the old standby for indoor training works well, there are other choices for indoor potties. Puppy pads can be used for Pugs of any age and can be inserted in a puppy pad tray for extra protection for your floor. The doggy version of the cat litter box is also available.

Basic Commands

Teaching your Pug basic commands will go much more smoothly if you adhere to the following guidelines:

- Pugs love praise, attention, and food—not necessarily in that order.
- Training time should be a fun activity that you and your Pug share.
- Use the Pug's natural desire for a treat or to be the centre of attention as part of the training process.
- As the training progresses, don't give

Being Good

a treat every time but do give praise. Eventually, the Pug will respond to the commands without expecting a treat.

- Commands should be spoken firmly and clearly. The Pug is not a breed that responds to a harsh voice or yelling.
- Be patient. Different dogs learn at a different pace.
- In the beginning, keep training time short, just a few minutes at a time each day so he doesn't get bored or frustrated. Remember to praise or reward him anytime he properly responds to a command. Once he understands what the command means, incorporate it into the daily schedule to reinforce his training.
- Be consistent. Use the same words or phrases so that the Pug can identify what action is associated with each command.
- Before you give a command, you must have your Pug's undivided attention. Hold a treat in front of him while saying, "Watch" or "Look at me" or by using a hand signal that conveys the same message. As he stares at you, praise him and give him the treat.
- Decide upon a release word that will let your Pug know when he can stop the commanded action. "Okay" or "All done" are some examples of release words.
- Training your Pug will be easier if you use a collar and lead to help guide him through learning each command.

If you find it difficult to teach the basic commands to your Pug, consider enrolling in a beginning obedience class. The trainer can evaluate your situation and make sure that both you and the Pug are following the correct procedure. As a bonus, trainers also share training tips based on their years of experience. Here's a tip a

Treats and Training

It's no secret—Pugs love to eat. This makes training with treats an easy way to get your Pug's attention and to motivate him to respond correctly. It's also no secret that the Pug is prone to obesity. Therefore, you must consider the size and type of treat that will be healthy for your Pug.

The size of the treat should be quite small, as the Pug is more interested in quantity rather than quality or size. Also consider the calorie count and if a treat is healthy. If you choose a commercial dog treat, go for the smallest size and one with a low calorie count. Other treats can be Cheerios, tiny pieces of cheese, pieces of carrot, etc.

Years ago I watched a segment about dog obesity on a television news programme. One of the owners of an obese dog confessed to the dog trainer that he gives his dog a whole slice of cheese for a snack or training treat. The aghast dog trainer explained that she could get 100 treats out of one slice of cheese!

You'll need your Pug's full attention to train him properly.

trainer shared with me, for dogs who will not listen to a firm vocal command: Don't yell at him—do the opposite. Speak so softly that his curiosity will make him come closer and focus his attention on you.

Sit

The "Sit" command will teach your Pug to have good manners. Pugs tend to jump up on people when they are overexcited, and common triggers are meal or snack time, preparing to go outside, or the arrival of visitors. It is much easier to prepare his meal or prevent him from jumping up on visitors if he is sitting down.

Stand in front of your Pug and get his attention by holding a treat in front of his nose. Then slowly raise the treat over his head while saying, "Sit." Your Pug will naturally sit as his eyes follow the treat passing over his head. Praise him by saying, "Good sit" followed by, "Good dog" (or good boy/girl/name). Then let him have the treat.

I've found that "sit" is the easiest command to teach. You can also reinforce this command outside of training sessions. Anytime you notice your Pug is ready to sit, say "Sit" followed by, "Good sit" when he completes the task.

Stay

The "Stay" command is not only a good manners behaviour but it can be an important safety command as well. For example, if your Pug wants a closer look as you deal with a pot boiling over in the kitchen, or someone leaves the front door open and your Pug is making a dash for it, saying "Stay" can be a lifesaver. A dog who responds to "Stay" will have a better chance of avoiding a dangerous mishap, either inside or outside of the home.

It may be easier for you to teach your Pug "Stay" in combination with the "Sit" command. Give the command to "Sit," praise or reward, then say, "Stay" as you hold your hand up with the palm facing your Pug's face. Slowly back away. If he stays, praise or reward. If he gets up before the release command, have him sit and start again. Be sure to give a release command such as "Okay" when you're finished, and praise or reward.

Come

The "Come" command is a practical way to have your dog come to you rather than having to hunt for him in the home or chase after him. Some Pugs may be very good at the "Come" command in the home but not when outside. At home, the Pug may not want to miss a tasty treat, a belly rub, or a nap on his owner's lap. However, the great outdoors presents all manner of distractions: intriguing sights, sounds and smells. Remember, the Pug was bred to be a companion dog, not a work dog, so he may become conveniently "hard of hearing" when he is too busy to heed your call. This is the primary reason that the Pug should be on lead or in a fenced-in area when outside.

Stand in front of your Pug, get his attention, and say, "Stay." Then back away a few feet, say his name and "Come." Reward him with a treat and praise when he reaches you. As you practice this command, lengthen the distance between you.

In order for your Pug to consistently obey the "Come" command, never use it when you are angry at him or plan to discipline him.

You can use a game of chase to reinforce the "Come" command. Letting him chase you can be a great help, but in the interest of safety never chase your dog. If a situation arises where your Pug is in danger, call his name with "Come" and run away from (not toward) him. It is more likely he will run back to you instead of toward danger. If you run after him, he may think it is a game and continue running away from you.

Down

The "Down" command should not be confused with "Off." "Down" means lie down; "Off" is the command to tell a dog to get down from furniture or from jumping up on a person. The "Down" command is used when you need your Pug to stay in one place for a period of time in a restful position. A Pug who has been taught to sit and to lie down will be well-mannered and easier to keep safe than an out-of-control dog.

Although one of the Pug's favourite positions is lying down for a nap, the "Down" command can be challenge for some Pugs. A Pug with a dominant personality may resist a command

SENIOR DOG TIP

Old Dogs and New Tricks

The Pug is so eager to please that even a senior Pug can learn new tricks or behaviours. Tailor training techniques for his mental and physical condition. Older Pugs are slower, so be patient. If he has hearing difficulties, use hand signals in combination with vocal commands. If the Pug has vision problems or is blind, gently guide him into the position or behaviour you want, give him a treat, and spend time petting him as a reward.

You can use a harness and lead instead of a collar to go for walks.

to take a submissive posture, yet on his own will roll over willing for a belly rub—a very submissive gesture. For this type of Pug, extra patience and consistent training will be necessary.

Begin by telling your Pug to "Sit," then praise or reward. Next, hold a treat under his nose and slowly lower it to the floor. Once he is lying down, give him praise and the treat.

An alternative method is to have him sit on your left side. Press down very lightly on his shoulders while moving a treat from his nose to the floor. Do *not* use force to push him down as that could cause injury. Remember, Pugs do not respond well to force.

Heel

How many times have you seen a large dog walking his person instead of the other way around? Now imagine how silly it looks to see a person being dragged along by a small dog! Pugs may be small but they are powerful, and any dog not properly trained can pull on his lead.

"Heel" is a formal way of saying

"Walk nicely on the lead." Begin with the Pug on your left side and the lead in your right hand. Say his name and "Heel" while walking forward. Praise him when he walks beside you. If he tries to go sideways, backward or doesn't move at all, give a gentle tug on the lead to lead him back into place. If he walks ahead of you, stop and cut the slack on the lead. Then begin again when he's back by your side.

Pugs are curious and social creatures. It is easy for them to get distracted when out for a walk. Practice, consistency, and patience are the keys to success.

Leave It

"Leave it" is one of the most valuable commands that I learned in obedience class. I use it often to teach my Pug what objects she is not allowed to touch, both within the home and outside. Also, consider this: what if you accidentally drop something on the floor and your Pug is right there ready to scoop it up into his mouth and eat it? If it is a small piece of a carrot stick, no harm done. But what if you drop a pill or other item that can be toxic or deadly to your Pug? What if

Being Good

you are out walking your Pug, and he has the desire to taste-test something disgusting before you

Only teach tricks your Pug seems comfortable with.

can pull him away? This is where the "Leave it" command comes in handy.

Put your Pug on a loose lead, toss a treat onto the floor, and give the command "Leave It." Gently tug the lead if he tries to get the treat. Praise him when he leaves the treat alone and give him a treat from your hand, *not the treat from the floor,* as a reward. You can further practice this by placing a treat on the floor for him "to find," say "Leave It," and reward him when he responds correctly with a treat from your hand.

Tricks

Pugs can be a problematic breed to teach tricks. Some Pugs are more athletic and limber and have an easier time with physical tricks. Other Pugs, based on age, condition, and weight, may not be able to do physically challenging tricks. Only teach tricks your Pug seems comfortable with.

Sometimes you can teach your Pug a trick with little effort. Most Pugs have an amusing behaviour that they do naturally. Catch him in the act, say a command to associate with that action, and then praise him enthusiastically. Only apply this technique to a behaviour that is safe and not a behaviour that should be discouraged. Here are two fun tricks you might want to try with your Pug.

The Waltzing Matilda

Teaching a dog to walk on his hind legs was probably one of the first dog tricks ever invented. I find it rather hilarious when my own Pug does it, because she only does it backwards—like Ginger Rogers waltzing with an invisible Fred Astaire. When she does it on her own, I say "Good waltz" to associate that action with a command and give her a treat when she's done.

84

Pugs

The Expert Knows

Finding a Trainer

There are several advantages to taking your Pug to a professional trainer. Instructors don't just train your dog and hand him back—you are learning the correct training methods along with your Pug. The trainer can evaluate any difficulties and work with you on solutions. Trainers can also share inside tips.

There are many ways to find a trainer for your Pug. Ask for recommendations from pet professionals: breeders, veterinarians, groomers, local animal shelters, and local pet shops. Some of these sources may even provide training at their locations. You can also check the Association of Pet Dog Trainers (APDT) website at www.aptd.co.uk to search for a trainer in your area.

Not all trainers are created equal, so ask around about the trainer's reputation and interview the trainer yourself. Visit the location where the trainer works. Is it clean? Do the trainer's own dogs seem happy, healthy, and well-behaved? Does the trainer use positive reinforcement and reward methods as opposed to punishment? How long has the trainer been in business? Is the trainer involved with other dog activities or clubs?

There are plenty of well-qualified trainers out there, so do your research and you'll be able to locate a good one.

Chapter **7**

In the
Doghouse

There are a number of factors that can contribute to problem behaviours in a dog. The easiest factor to remedy is often ignored—the need for training. Although the Pug was bred for companionship, he wasn't born with the knowledge that you do not want him to use your Persian rug for a toilet, or to lie on your expensive silk-covered chair chewing on his saliva covered toy. It's up to you to teach him proper behaviour patiently and calmly. Yelling and screaming will only acerbate the problem, not solve it.

If a dog is lonely, bored, or feels ignored, he may act out inappropriately, such as constant barking or shredding your newspapers. He may do this to get your attention or even just for something to do to occupy his time. More serious factors that may cause behaviour problems include: undiagnosed and/or untreated health issues; temperament problems from poor breeding; or abuse.

Making the Adjustment

A Pug who is new to your home, even if he had been previously trained, will need time to adjust to his new surroundings. Confusion or anxiety may lead to a temporary lapse in housetraining habits or in following known commands. He also needs to learn about his new surroundings: what rooms he is allowed to be in or not be in; which furniture he may or may not get up on; and where his designated potty area is located. Your home and neighbourhood is filled with new sights, sounds, and smells, and this can be both exciting and confusing to a new dog.

You also need to consider the Pug's past experience or, in some cases, the lack of it. For instance, if your Pug came from a home in which he never climbed up and down a staircase,

this new experience can be frightening for him. My own Pug came into my life at nine-months of age. Her breeder informed me that the she had never climbed stairs before, and explained that I would have to be patient while she learned this new action. For the first week that I had my Pug, I could only coax her up the bottom level of the stairs. Once she reached the stair just before the midway landing, she would stop as if a force field was preventing her from continuing her journey. No amount of coaxing or treats could lure her one simple step up to the landing. Then I would have to carry her up the rest of the way.

One evening I left my Pug downstairs while I had dinner upstairs with my parents. She had tried to follow me but once again could not get past the center landing. Listening to her whimpering on the stairs while my family had dinner was heartbreaking. All of a sudden we heard her make a loud "woo-woo" sound as she gathered up her courage and ran up all the stairs

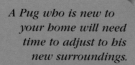

A Pug who is new to your home will need time to adjust to his new surroundings.

Finding a Behaviourist

If you are having a behaviour issue with your dog, and your veterinarian has ruled out a physical or medical problem as the source, your next step may be to consult a dog trainer. If the dog trainer's efforts are unsuccessful, or if he or she informs you that the problem is beyond the scope of dog training, then your next step is find an animal behaviourist.

An animal behaviourist is not the same as a dog trainer. An animal behaviourist is someone who has studied the science of animal behaviour, which delves deeply into understanding why animals do what they do.

Ask your veterinarian if he or she knows of a qualified animal behaviourist. Your veterinarian may prefer an animal behaviourist who has a veterinary degree, as he or she can also dispense medication if it is needed. The Association of Pet Behaviour Counsellors (APBC) is a good resource for finding certified behaviourists. Not all qualified animal behaviourists are veterinarians, but do not overlook those who have years of experience and success at correcting problem behaviours.

A visit to an animal behaviourist usually includes taking a history of the problem behaviour, observing how the family and pet interact, evaluating the problem, devising a treatment plan, and discussing the prognosis. Remember, the prognosis is based on the assumption that the family will follow through with the at-home instructions that are part of the treatment plan.

for the first time in her life. After that, she never had a problem going up and down the stairs.

Another obstacle that may confuse a new dog is your flooring if it is different from what he is used to. For instance, hardwood or tile floors may feel slippery to him if he is used to carpeting. My Pug has a fear of wooden decks because she can see down in the space between the wooden slats. When I first brought her out onto our deck, she panicked. What I considered a teeny opening probably seemed like the Grand Canyon to her. We resolved the problem by covering the deck with an inexpensive piece of indoor/outdoor carpeting. After that, she always enjoyed sharing good times on the deck with her human family.

Some adopted or rescued Pugs may have always been kept inside, caged, or only exposed to concrete surfaces. These Pugs, who had never been exposed to a grassy landscape, may find the sensation of standing on grass for the first time to be confusing or frightening. Reassurance and patience will help most new Pugs adapt more easily to their unfamiliar surroundings.

If a problem persists, have your veterinarian examine your Pug to determine whether or not the root cause is physical. If the problem is not

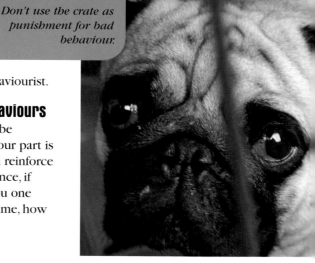

Don't use the crate as punishment for bad behaviour.

physical, then you may want to consult a dog trainer or an animal behaviourist.

Dealing With Problem Behaviours

Owners need to set rules and be consistent. Inconsistency on your part is confusing to your Pug and can reinforce a problem behaviour. For instance, if nipping elicits a laugh from you one time and then anger another time, how

SENIOR DOG TIP

Breaking Old Habits

The longer we practice a bad habit, the harder it is to break it. The same holds true for dogs. Perhaps you have adopted an older Pug with undesirable habits. Or maybe you put off correcting that sweet puppy and now that he is an adult or senior, his problems aren't so cute anymore. It will take time and patience to change an older dog's behaviour. However, you do have one thing going for you with the Pug breed—his love for food and attention. Any training method that involves a food reward and his owner's undivided attention is sure to get your Pug interested. Be consistent, and you will see rewards.

is your Pug going to learn which is the correct behaviour? From a dog's point of view, nipping is playful. He will probably continue nipping because he hasn't made the connection that nipping a person is inappropriate.

Dogs need to learn what behaviours are inappropriate and be redirected to perform correct behaviours. Lots of praise should ensue when the Pug behaves properly. If your Pug is being stubborn and won't follow a command, ignore him for a few minutes. The Pug can't stand to be ignored and may do an about-face to regain your favour and attention.

Another way to redirect behaviour is to clap your hands or use a shake can. A shake can is made from any empty can with just enough pennies or rocks inside to make a loud rattle. If you catch him doing something inappropriate, shake the can, and do not let the Pug see where the noise is coming from. The noise will startle him and arouse his curiosity, which will interrupt the behaviour you are trying to stop. Once

Pugs

he has stopped the offending behaviour, praise him for being a good dog.

Yelling in anger at any dog is not the way to change his behaviour patterns. Yelling is negative attention, and to most dogs, negative attention is better than no attention. It may also create anxiety that contributes to negative behaviour, or in the case of a Pug who is stubborn, reinforce negative behaviour. Proper training and consistency, along with patience and reward (praise or treat) are the most effective means of turning your bad dog into a good dog.

Begging

Begging can be one of the Pug's worst habits if he is allowed to get away with it. The Pug will beg for food and for your attention. Remember, the Pug's favourite two things in the world are you and food. He must learn that "No" means no. If he knows that you may give in if he pesters you long enough, you will never be able to stop him from begging.

I have my Pug on a food schedule, including her snack times. Usually, you can set your watch by her inner clock. She knows exactly when it is meal or snack time, and she makes no bones about reminding me. However, she will try to convince me from time to time that an early snack would be lovely. I taught her the phrase "It's not time yet." I use that phrase consistently and without giving in. As soon as I utter those magic words, she stops begging.

Barking (Excessive)

The Pug may bark occasionally, but this is not a breed known for problem barking. Barking is natural for dogs, and your Pug may bark when he hears other dogs barking. It doesn't matter if it's the neighbourhood dog or a dog on TV—the call of the wild is hard to resist. And there are times you may want your Pug to bark, such as when someone is at the door. However, a dog who barks continuously can be a nuisance to both the owner and the neighbours.

FAMILY-FRIENDLY TIP

Keeping Kids Safe

Children need to be taught how to interact safely with dogs and other pets. If it is the family Pug that is displaying a behaviour issue, the child should be informed of the problem in terms that match the child's comprehension level. Then clearly explain the safety rules for interacting with the dog. The safety rules should protect both the child and the Pug.

If the child is too young to understand or not mature enough to follow safety precautions, then the child should not have access to the dog without adult supervision. Children should also learn never to approach an unknown dog without its owner's permission.

In the Doghouse

> *The Pug is not usually a "barky" breed, but any dog can persist in excessive barking if bored or lonely.*

Problem barking may be caused by boredom, the need for attention, or separation anxiety. Other breeds may bark because they are territorial, but the Pug may bark because he feels left out of the fun. More mental and physical stimulation can help curb his boredom. He may need more quality time and attention from his owner. Try an extra walk after dinner or some fun in the park on the weekends.

You can also teach your Pug a command to stop barking. While your Pug is barking, in a firm and calm voice say, "Quiet." Praise him when he ceases barking. If he ignores the command and continues barking, distract him from what he is barking at and immediately praise him when he stops. If that doesn't work, try a time out in his crate; but remember, the crate is not for punishment. Let him have a toy to help settle him down.

Jumping Up

Jumping up is a very common behaviour with the Pug. He will jump up to greet you, to get your attention, or to see if what you're holding is edible. You may not mind if your Pug jumps up on you (as he can only reach about knee-level), but the sociable Pug will greet everyone that way, including strangers. While it is hard to imagine, not everyone is as enamoured of your Pug as you are.

Teach your Pug the "Off" command to stop this behaviour. Do not say, "Down" as that is the command that means *lie down*. As you say, "Off," gently twist away from him, so he has to let go. Do not hit him or push him. Just move enough so that he gets off. Then praise him when he is calm and standing.

Trying to prevent the behaviour before it starts can also help. If you know that your Pug is getting ready to jump up on someone, give him the command, "Sit." This will take practice, and he may have an occasional relapse—especially when the excitement of greeting a visitor is just too much for him.

Chewing

Dogs need to chew, but they must be taught what is appropriate to chew and what is off limits. Choose chew toys for your Pug that are size appropriate. Also examine toys for safety, making sure there aren't parts that can be torn off and swallowed. Don't give your Pug something that is similar to an item that is off limits—he won't know the difference between an old shoe and your new Manolo Blahniks.

If your Pug insists on chewing an object that can't be removed from his reach, such as a piece of furniture, use a spray that tastes bitter. These sprays can be found in pet shops, and the bitter taste will discourage chewing.

Nipping

To a dog, nipping is a natural part of play. He doesn't understand that the playful nipping he did with his littermates can injure a human playmate. All dogs, including the Pug, must be taught that nipping and biting will not be tolerated.

Teach your Pug the command, "No bite." When he nips you, say the command firmly and stop playing with him for a few minutes. Resume playing and praise him for

Jumping up is a very common behaviour with the Pug.

Anxiety and Aggression

If your Pug is displaying aggression or if he is suffering from severe separation anxiety, it is time to seek professional help.

Aggressive behaviour in any dog is a potential danger to family members, as well as to everyone else who comes into contact with that dog. Children and other pets are especially vulnerable. Pugs are rarely aggressive or dangerous, but there are exceptions. Aggressive biting is unusual in the Pug breed, and it needs to be evaluated immediately by a professional.

Separation anxiety can happen with dogs like the Pug, who crave being around their human family. While some Pugs will use their alone time to catch a nap, other Pugs become anxious when their owner is out-of-sight. When a Pug suffering from separation anxiety is left alone, he goes into full panic mode and may become a danger to himself or to your property. Out-of-control separation anxiety may manifest in the following ways: physical problems such as breathing difficulties or inappropriate toileting; incessant barking that has your neighbours complaining; or as destructive behaviour such as destroying furniture or possessions. He could get hurt if he goes on a rampage or if his anxiety triggers a serious respiratory event. Seek professional help at once.

playing nicely. If he nips again, repeat the command and ignore him for a few minutes. If he continues nipping, place him in his crate for a short while. Always remember to praise him when he behaves properly.

Digging

The Pug isn't a serious digger like terrier breeds. His curiosity may cause him to scratch just below the surface, but chances are he won't dig a deep hole. He may dig out a patch of grass so that he can roll on the cooler layer of dirt beneath it. He may do this to cool down on a warm day, to relieve an itch, or because it feels good and it's fun.

However, there is an exception to every rule, and some Pugs may be expert diggers who can tunnel an escape route under the fence. If your Pug is doing some serious digging, you'll want to teach him a command to stop.

In a firm and calm voice say, "No dig." If he doesn't respond, which is quite possible if he is having a good time, you may have to pick him up and designate an area in the garden where he can dig and roll around to his heart's content.

If your Pug has had plenty of exercise, he will be less likely to dig. If he continues to dig in a spot that must be discouraged, bury some of his stool in that spot. Most dogs will not dig up their own waste.

Housesoiling

Housesoiling needs to be approached in a very different way than the other behaviours mentioned in this chapter. The first step in correcting housesoiling or inappropriate toileting is to understand *why* your Pug is having potty accidents. Ask yourself the following questions:

- Was your Pug properly housetrained?
- Is he allowed access to his potty area, especially if it is outside, frequently enough? Puppies and senior Pugs need more frequent potty breaks.
- Is he new to the house? A new Pug may be confused by the different surroundings, and he will need to learn where his potty area is located.
- Is he healthy? He may have eaten something that gave him diarrhoea,

No one likes to think about losing their dog, but it can happen— especially with the resourceful and intelligent Pug.

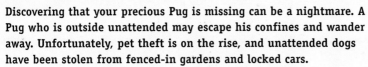

Finding the Lost Pug

Discovering that your precious Pug is missing can be a nightmare. A Pug who is outside unattended may escape his confines and wander away. Unfortunately, pet theft is on the rise, and unattended dogs have been stolen from fenced-in gardens and locked cars.

Time is of the essence if your Pug goes missing. Keep a current photograph of your Pug that can be used on a "Lost Dog" poster. List any unusual markings or traits that can help identify him. Offer a cash reward as it may increase the chances that someone will come forward with information. Posters should be visible and readable to passing cars as well as pedestrians. Place the posters in at least a five mile radius from where the dog went missing.

Contact all the following from the surrounding towns in case your Pug shows up at one of these facilities: animal control offices, police departments, veterinarian surgeries and hospitals, animal shelters, and Pug rescue organizations.

Talk to people in the area where your Pug went missing: neighbours, pedestrians, shopkeepers and so on.

If you have exhausted all local avenues, extend your search area outward. There are also websites that include "Lost and Found" pet information.

Last but not least, don't give up! Persistence may eventually lead to recovering your Pug.

and he was unable to make it to his potty area. Or a urinary tract infection or other medical issue could be the culprit. Take him to the vet for a checkup.

- Has there been a change in the household? Instability or turmoil in the home, such as frequent arguments or yelling, can make a dog anxious and nervous, which can lead to potty accidents.

Once you've determined the cause, you can start working on the solution.

If your Pug does have an accident, never yell at him or push his nose into the mess. He won't make the connection as to why you are so angry, and it is bound to frighten him. This method sets him up for future failure by creating a confused and anxious dog.

Your Pug did *not* have an accident just to annoy you. If the potty accidents aren't temporary, and you have exhausted all the above possibilities, he may just need a refresher course in housetraining. Start from scratch, be calm and patient, and praise him when he relieves himself in the proper place.

Chapter 8

Stepping Out

Going out with your Pug doesn't have to be limited to walks or playing in the garden. There are organised activities available that you and your Pug can share with other people and dogs. There are sports such as obedience, agility, and freestyle. You and your Pug can train for the Canine Good Citizen Scheme or become a certified therapy dog team. If your dog meets the Pug breed standard, you may want to compete in dog shows to see if he has the right stuff to become a champion.

I f you prefer leisurely travelling the back roads and highways, take your Pug with you. He will enjoy the adventure as well as spending time with you. The increase in pet-friendly lodging is making it easier to include your Pug in holiday plans.

Whether it is playing in your own back garden or travelling around the country, spending time with your Pug is fun and strengthens the bond between you.

Show dogs are judged by how close they come to the breed standard.

Sports and Activities

Certain breeds are associated with and excel at specific sports because it is what they were bred to do. There are breeds that hunt or herd, run like the wind, swim, retrieve, or protect. If you think that the only sport your companion Pug can compete in is "World's Greatest Couch Potato," think again. Not to be outdone by their larger or faster canine brethren, Pugs are now competing in agility and winning high marks. Obedience and freestyle are two other sports that you can pursue with your Pug. Or if you're not interested in athletic events, you can compete in dog shows, give back to the community by doing therapy work, or just plain have some fun in your back garden with your best friend.

Canine Good Citizen

If you and your Pug enjoy training together, you may want to consider having him tested for the Canine Good Citizen Scheme. The Canine Good Citizen (CGC) Scheme was developed by the Kennel Club (KC) to promote responsible pet ownership and reward dogs who demonstrate good manners. The programme is open to both pure-bred and mixed breeds.

The CGC test determines how well your dog responds to various commands. Dogs who pass the test earn their CGC title.

Showing (Conformation)

Dog shows (conformation events) allow pure-bred dogs to strut their stuff in the conformation ring. While the uninitiated may assume this is just a canine beauty contest, it is actually a vital component in determining the future of the breed.

In the United Kingdom, the KC sets the breed standards—the written guideline for each pure-bred dog breed that describes the ideal dog. Reputable breeders strive to match their breed

98

Pugs

standard as closely as possible. While no dog is perfect, the dogs who most closely match the standard are awarded points in the conformation ring toward a championship title. Champion show dogs are the shining examples of their breed in both build and temperament. The conformation ring also provides a place where breeders can determine if their breeding programme is on track.

Match shows are practice shows for dogs and people new to the sport. The dogs are judged, rosettes are handed out, but there are no points awarded. The real deal is the Challenge Certificate show in which the goal is to earn points towards a dog's championship.

In the first stage, dogs of the same breed compete against each other in designated classes, and each class is divided by gender. The common terminology used to indicate the gender of a dog is to use the word *dog* for a male and *bitch* for a female. Winners in each class go on to compete against each other for Winners Dog and Winners Bitch, and points are awarded for these titles. The Winners Dog and Winners Bitch go on to compete along side Champion dogs; this stage combines both genders and colour varieties in the ring. The very best example of a Pug conforming to the standard wins the title Best of Breed. There are seven dog groups designated by the KC: Gundog, Hound, Working, Terrier, Toy, Utility, and Pastoral. All the Best of Breed dogs compete against the other breeds within their group. The Pug is part of the Toy group, which currently consists of 21 breeds, including the Pekingese, Chihuahua, Yorkshire Terrier, Cavalier King Charles Spaniel, Chinese Crested, and the Italian Greyhound. From among this diverse group, the Group winner for First place is chosen. The seven Group winners then compete for the coveted title Best in Show.

Registered Name Versus Call Name

If you've watched a dog show on television, you may have noticed that each dog has a rather long, fancy, or unusual name. This is the dog's *registered name*. A kennel name is often incorporated into the registered name. The *call name* is the actual name that the dog is called in his day to day life. For example, Kendoric's Riversong

Ch. Kendoric's Riversong Mulroney is the top winning Pug in the history of the breed.

Mulroney is called Dermot. The former name is his registered name, and the latter is his call name. Kendoric is the kennel line from which Dermot is descended, and Riversong is the kennel name of his owner. Dermot has earned his championship title, so now the abbreviation *CH* or *Ch.* precedes his registered name—Ch. Kendoric's Riversong Mulroney.

Sports

Agility

Agility is a very athletic sport for both the dog and his handler. In an agility

competition, each dog runs an obstacle course that includes a dog walk, seesaw, A-frame, tunnels, jumps, and weave poles. The sequence of the obstacle course changes for each competition, so the handler must learn the new sequence of the obstacles and direct the dog. The handler gets quite a workout too as he or she must keep up with the dog and cue him to perform the next obstacle. The winner is the dog who runs the fastest time with the fewest mistakes.

Have your veterinarian evaluate your Pug to determine if he is healthy enough for agility training and competing. Though some Pugs take to agility like a duck to water, others may experience breathing difficulties due to exertion, or may have previously undiagnosed health issues such as hip dysplasia or luxating patella.

Freestyle

Don't have a partner for the Saturday night dance? Look no further than your Pug! Freestyle (also known as "Dancing with Dogs") combines dance and dog training. Each team, comprised of handler and dog, performs a choreographed routine to music. Wearing costumes is part of the fun.

Extra patience may be needed to teach your Pug a freestyle routine compared to other breeds. Weave some of his natural moves into the routine and be aware of the limitations of his body type. A freestyle competition can be serious business, but it also should be fun.

Some canine freestyle routines involve fun costumes.

Obedience

The obedience competition demonstrates that dogs can be well-trained, have good manners, and can work as a team with their human handlers. A judge measures how well each dog follows his handler's commands while performing a specified routine. The commands are the same as those learned in a basic obedience class, plus some additional more complicated commands. Come, sit, stay, down, and heel commands are used, and more intricate moves include hand signals, retrieving, and scent discrimination.

Therapy

Do you and your Pug enjoy meeting people and spreading cheer? Are you looking for a way to help others? Then you may want to consider having your Pug certified as a therapy dog. Therapy dogs visit hospitals, nursing homes, and other institutions to give comfort and companionship to the patients. Therapy dogs are also used to bring comfort to victims of disaster.

The Pug's personality is a natural for a therapy dog as he loves people and interacting with them. However, not all Pugs may be cut out to be therapy dogs—especially if a dog is too shy or aggressive around strangers or too rambunctious. Therapy animals come in all shapes and sizes, but the Pug's size makes him an ideal lap dog.

A dog must pass a process, like the one outlined by Pets As Therapy (PAT) in order to become a therapy dog. The first step is to earn his Canine Good Citizen title, then he must pass additional

Sports and Safety

Although the Pug was bred solely to be a companion, there are Pugs who have the energy, stamina, and drive to compete in a dog sport. A healthy and energetic Pug who loves to play would probably do well in a canine sport. Match his favourite at-home activities with a sport that has similar activity.

Before beginning a new athletic programme, have your veterinarian determine if your Pug is healthy enough for the activity in which you are interested. You want to verify that your Pug doesn't have a hidden or undiagnosed condition that would be seriously aggravated by strenuous activity.

Seek out a qualified trainer in the sport so that you and your Pug can learn the sport properly and safely.

requirements which are tested by a therapy evaluator.

Volunteering as part of a therapy dog team can be one of the most rewarding activities that you can share with your Pug.

Fun and Games

Treat Ball Soccer

My favourite game with my Pug is "treat ball soccer." It began as a way to exercise my Pug indoors during a blustery New England winter with a stretch of sub-zero temperatures and a wind chill factor that took my breath away. I feared for my Pug's safety in such extreme weather.

The only equipment you need for this game is a small treat ball and some treats to put inside it. Stuffable treat balls are available at any pet shop—the one I use is approximately 3 inches (7.6 cm) in diameter. Put about six to ten small treats in the ball. Use low-calorie, non-fat dog treats or some other healthy snack—I use Cheerios because my dog trainer recommended them for training treats.

Once the treats are in the ball, you can just roll it on the floor and watch your Pug chase it and bat it around to get the treats to fall out. However, I have added a twist which provides my Pug with more exercise and amuses me to no end. I roll the ball under the dining room table and watch as my Pug leaps like a gazelle over the chair rungs. If the ball ricochets off a table leg into another direction, my Pug can stop on a dime, whirl around, and resume the chase. She scarfs down each piece of cereal as soon as it is released from the ball (just in case a pack of hungry wolves are preparing to steal it from her).

Hide & Seek

This game is appealing to puppies and has an educational aspect. Have someone hold the puppy while you hide in another room—but make sure you are easy to find at first. Then call the puppy by name with the command "Come." Let the puppy find you and praise him or give him a treat. As he catches on to the game, you can start "hiding" in more difficult places. The great thing about playing this game is that your Pug is also learning to come when called.

Travel and Holidays

A benefit to owning a small dog is that it is easier to travel with him. His doggy supplies and the amount of food you have to transport take up far less room

Pugs

FAMILY-FRIENDLY TIP

Safe Travelling

Travelling with both children and pets can be a challenge. Safety should always be the number one concern for both the child and Pug. When travelling by car, children must wear seat belts, and babies must be placed in rear-facing car seats to avoid serious injury in the event of an accident. Your Pug should be protected too by placing him in a well-ventilated travel crate or by restraining him in a seat belt system created specifically for dogs. The crate is a better option for long trips and will also provide a calm and private environment for your Pug. Bring along toys or games that can amuse the child when the Pug needs a nap or peace and quiet.

> *Your Pug will love to explore new places.*

than a large breed dog.

To locate pet-friendly lodging, contact the Visitor's Information Centre where you will be staying. There is also much useful information available on the internet. Always call ahead before making a reservation to double-check that your lodging is pet-friendly even if it listed as such on a website or in a brochure. Also, don't assume that because you could bring your Pug to a particular place in the past that pets are still welcome. Policies for hotels, inns, and rental properties can change from one season to the next.

By Car

Dogs should be restrained or crated when riding in a car. If there is an accident, a loose dog can be injured or killed and may also injure others in the car, including the driver. Even just swerving the car to avoid an accident can turn a loose dog into a dangerous projectile. A dog who is loose in the front passenger seat is also at risk for a serious or fatal injury if the air bag deploys.

There are pet safety harnesses available for travelling with your dog, which connect to the seat belt.

By Air

If your dog needs to travel by plane, you'll need a travel crate that meets airline requirements. Most Pugs are small enough to travel in the cabin, and there are travel crates available for small dogs that can be put under the seat in the passenger section of the plane. Always check with the specific airline you are flying on to verify the size and type of crate that meets their requirements. Be aware that a larger size Pug might not fit in the size crate that is allowed in the passenger cabin.

Packing Your Pug's Suitcase

Packing your Pug's supplies for a trip may seem overwhelming at first, but with experience you will eventually have a system that works well for you. A good starting point is to make a list of the things your Pug uses or needs on a typical day. Highlight important items, such as medication, that may not be available at your destination. Once everything is on paper, it will be easier to determine what must be packed versus what can be left behind or purchased at your destination.

Stepping Out

The following list contains some of the items you may want to consider bringing with you:

- **Crate:** The crate should be lined with a mattress pad, towel, or blanket for your Pug's comfort. A travel crate can provide safety while travelling

by car and double as a familiar place to rest or sleep when living away from home.

- **Water and water bowl:** Bottled water will ensure that your Pug has fresh water while travelling and at your destination if the tap water is substandard. Detachable water bowls are available for crates.
- **Food and food bowl:** If you use commercial food or specialised ingredients for your Pug's meals, bring enough along in case it is not available at your destination. The same goes for treats and supplements.
- **Collar, lead, harness, ID tags:** Bring a spare set along in case one set gets dirty or damaged.
- **Bedding:** A crate can double for a bed, or another option is to bring a dog bed along. If you choose to have your Pug sleep with you, remember that you are a guest, whether paying for accommodations or staying at a private home. Bring a blanket or pad to cover the area on the bed where your Pug will sleep to keep the bedding clean and protect it from accidental soiling.
- **Medications:** Bring both veterinarian prescribed and over-the-counter medications.
- **First-aid kit:** First Aid kits can be purchased ready-made, or you can make your own. (See Chapter 5 for the contents of a first-aid kit.)
- **Grooming and bathing:** Pack his hair brush and flea comb. Doggy bath wipes are a handy way to keep your Pug clean while on the road. Don't forget supplies for ear, eye, and dental

SENIOR DOG TIP

Tips for Travelling With Your Senior Pug

- For a senior Pug who is experiencing the aches and pains that can accompany old age, provide a cushier crate pad or blanket while travelling by car to absorb the road bumps.
- In hot weather, remember that Pugs of all ages are susceptible to overheating, but it can be worse for the older Pug. Use the air conditioner in your car or lodging and seek the shade when outside.
- In cold weather it is advisable to preheat the car to protect your Pug from becoming chilled.
- Always keep fresh water on hand while travelling.
- If your senior Pug is on medication or a special diet, be sure to bring enough to last for the duration of the trip.

Pugs

care. Also pack nail clippers or a nail grinder and an emery board.

- **Potty**: Carry baggies to pick up messes after your Pug relieves himself outside. Keep a stain and odour remover on hand for potty accidents indoors or in the car. If your Pug is paper trained, bring his doggy pads or newspaper.

- **Toys and chews**: Favourite toys and chews provide comfort, prevent boredom, and may also alleviate any anxiety associated with an unfamiliar environment.

- **Current photo/"lost dog" signs**: Before your trip, make signs that include a current photo of your Pug. This can be easily done on computer. If no one will be at your home during your travels, arrange with a relative, friend, or your veterinarian to use

their phone number as the contact number on the poster, should your

Pug get lost. Include your mobile phone number if you have one. The phone number where you are staying can be added later with a marking pen.

- **In case of emergency**: Bring your veterinarian's phone number with you in case he or she needs to provide vital information if something unforeseen happens to your Pug. If possible, find out what veterinarian or animal hospital is closest to your travel destination.

105

Stepping Out

With planning and preparation, you won't have to leave your Pug behind!

Resources

Associations and Organisations

American Kennel Club (AKC)
5580 Centerview Drive
Raleigh, NC 27606
Telephone: (919) 233-9767
Fax: (919) 233-3627
E-mail: info@akc.org
www.akc.org

Canadian Kennel Club (CKC)
89 Skyway Avenue, Suite 100
Etobicoke, Ontario M9W 6R4
Telephone: (416) 675-5511
Fax: (416) 675-6506
E-mail: information@ckc.ca
www.ckc.ca

Federation Cynologique Internationale (FCI)
Secretariat General de la FCI
Place Albert 1er, 13
B – 6530 Thuin
Belqique
www.fci.be

The Kennel Club
1 Clarges Street
London
W1J 8AB
Telephone: 0870 606 6750
Fax: 0207 518 1058
www.the-kennel-club.org.uk

United Kennel Club (UKC)
100 E. Kilgore Road
Kalamazoo, MI 49002-5584
Telephone: (269) 343-9020
Fax: (269) 343-7037
E-mail: pbickell@ukcdogs.com
www.ukcdogs.com

Pet Sitters

National Association of Registered Petsitters
www.dogsit.com

UK Petsitters
www.ukpetsitter.com

Rescue Organisations and Animal Welfare Groups

British Veterinary Association Animal Welfare Foundation
7 Mansfield Street
London W1G 9NQ
Telephone: 0207 436 2970
Email: bva-awf@bva.co.uk
www.bva-awf.org.uk

Dogs Trust
17 Wakley Street
London
EC1V 7RQ
Telephone: 0207 837 0006
www.dogstrust.org.uk

Royal Society for the Prevention of Cruelty to Animals (RSPCA)
Telephone: 0870 3335 999
Fax: 0870 7530 284
www.rspca.org.uk

Scottish Society for the Prevention of Cruelty to Animals (SSPCA)
Braehead Mains, 603
Queensferry Road
Edinburgh EH4 6EA
Telephone: 0131 339 4777
Email: enquiries@scottishspca.org
www.scottishspca.org

Pugs

Sports

Canine Freestyle Federation, Inc.
Secretary: Brandy Clymire
E-Mail: secretary@canine-freestyle.org
www.canine-freestyle.org

International Agility Link (IAL)
Global Administrator: Steve Drinkwater
E-mail: yunde@powerup.au
www.agilityclick.com

World Canine Freestyle Organisation
P.O. Box 350122
Brooklyn, NY 11235-2525
Telephone: (718) 332-8336
www.worldcaninefreestyle.org

Therapy

Pets As Therapy
3a Grange Farm Cottages
Wycombe Road
Saunderton
Princes Risborough
Bucks HP27 9NS
www.petsastherapy.org

Training

Association of Pet Dog Trainers (APDT)
PO Box 17
Kampsford GL7 4W7
Telephone: 01285 810 811

Association of Pet Behaviour Counsellors
PO Box 46
Worcester WR8 9YS
Telephone: 01386 750743
Email:: info@apbc.org.uk
www.apbc.org.uk

Veterinary and Health Resources

British Veterinary Association (BVA)
7 Mansfield Street
London
W1G 9NQ
www.bva.co.uk

British Veterinary Hospitals Association (BHVA)
Station Bungalow
Main Road, Stockfield
Northumberland NE43 7HJ
Telephone: 07966 901619
www.BVHA.org.uk

Royal College of Veterinary Surgeons (RCVS)
Belgravia House
62-64 Horseferry Road
London SW1P 2AF
Telephone: 0207 222 2001
www.rcvs.org.uk

Association of Chartered Physiotherapists Specialising in Animal Therapy (ACPAT)
52 Littleham Road
Exmouth, Devon EX8 2QJ
Telephone: 01395 270648
www.acpat.org.uk

Association of British Veterinary Acupuncturists (ABVA)
66A Easthorpe, Southwell
Nottinghamshire NG25 0HZ
www.abva.co.uk

Publications

Books

Sara John
The Puppy Pack
Interpet Publishing 2008

Susan M Ewing
The Pug
Interpet Publishing 2008

Dominique De Vito
Training Your Dog
Interpet Publishing, 2007

Nester, Mary Ann
Agility Dog Training
Interpet Publishing, 2007

O'Neill
What Dog?
Interpet Publishing, 2006

Harvey, Su
Good Pup, Good Dog
Interpet Publishing, 2007

Evans, J M
What If My Dog?
Interpet Publishing, 2006

Tennant, Colin
Mini Encyclopedia of Dog Training & Behaviour
Interpet Publishing, 2005

Barnes, Julia
Living With A Rescued Dog
Interpet Publishing, 2004

Evans, J M & White, Kay
Doglopaedia
Ringpress Books, 1998

Evans, J M
Book of The Bitch
Ringpress Books, 1998

Magazines

Dogs Monthly
Ascot HouseHigh Street, Ascot,Berkshire
SL5 7JG
www.corsini.co.uk/dogsmonthly

Dog World
Somerfield House
Wotton Road, Ashford
Kent TN23 6LW
www.dogworld.co.uk

Dogs Today
Town Mill, Bagshot Road
Chobham
Surrey GU24 8BZ
Email: enquiries@dogstodaymagazine.co.uk
www.dogstodaymagazine.co.uk

Kennel Gazette
Kennel Club
1 Clarges Street
London W1J 8AB
www.thekennelclub.co.uk

K9 Magazine
21 High Street
Warsop
Nottinghamshire NG20 0AA
Email: mail@k9magazine.com
www.k9magazine.com

Our Dogs
Our Dogs Publishing
5 Oxford Road
Station Approach
Manchester
M60 1SX
www.ourdogs.co.uk

Your Dog
Roebuck House
33 Broad Street
Stamford
Lincolnshire PE9 1RB
www.yourdog.co.uk

Pugs

Index

109

Index

111

Index

Dedication

For my sister, Raine Phoenix, who encouraged me to get a companion dog; for my parents, Russell and Mary Ann Bourgeois, who truly believe that my Pug is their granddaughter; and for Guinevere (Keledor's Waltzing Matilda), my furbaby, muse, and Puggie soul-mate.

Acknowledgements

Many thanks to Doris Aldrich (Kendoric Pugs) and Janet Wilkinson (Windsor Pugs) for their expert advice and friendship. Thank you to Carolyn Koch (Riversong Pugs), Alan Alford, Darlene Arden, Luci Adams, Kate Enderlin and Chale Phoenix. Many thanks to Carien Van Gelder for attending dog shows with me. To the members of the Patriot Pug Dog Club and Pug Rescue of New England, thank you for your support, friendship and Pug education. Thank you to Patt Kolesar (*Pug Talk* magazine) for my first opportunity to become a dog writer. Thank you to my editor, Heather Russell-Revesz and the team at T.F.H. Publications. A very special thank you to Dorothy Kelly (Keledor Pugs) for my lovely Pug, Guinevere.

About the Author

Dianne Bourgeois is a contributing writer for *Pug Talk* magazine which carries her humor column "Pug Tales" about life with her Pug, Guinevere. She is the editor of *Pug Phoenix*, the newsletter for Pug Rescue of New England which also includes her column "Pet Pug Corner." Her columns "Pug Tales" and "Pet Pug Corner" have both received certificates of nomination in the Dog Writers Association of America annual writing competition. Dianne is a member of the Dog Writers Association of America, the Patriot Pug Dog Club, Pug Rescue of New England, and the Red Hat Society. She lives in Massachusetts with her family and her beloved Pug.

Photo Credits

Doris Aldrich: 61
Dianne Bourgeois: 16, 24, 49, 83
Laurie Capone: 75 (bottom)
Carol Carbone: 9, 68
Martin Carlsson Photography (Shutterstock): 76, 105
Judy Chandler: 103
Candice Cunningham (Shutterstock): 12, 55
Ross Daily (Shutterstock): 92
Tara Darling: 105 (top)
Lisa Eastman (Shutterstock): 65
Rachael Grazias (Shutterstock): 50
Alison Grippo (Shutterstock): 88
Daniel Hughes (Shutterstock): 8
Barry G. Hurt (Shutterstock): 90
Holly Jagger: 100
Carolyn Koch: 99
Dennis Ku (Shutterstock): 36

Franziska Lang (Shutterstock): 10
Carrieann Larmore (Shutterstock): 14, 70
Kate Nichols: 64
Chin Kit Sen (Shutterstock): 37
Gordon Snell (Shutterstock): 26, 85
Tiburon Studios (Shutterstock): 57
Christine Tanner (Shutterstock): 96
G. Tibbets (Shutterstock): 86
Bartosz Wardzinski (Shutterstock): 4, 23
Meredith & Eric Webb: 69, silhouette on pages 22, 67, 89, 93, 95
Janet Wilkinson: 58, 93
Paul S. Wolf (Shutterstock): 78

Cover: Franziska Lang (Shutterstock)
All other photos courtesy of Isabelle Francais